INTEGRATIVE PREACHING

Abingdon Preacher's Library

INTEGRATIVE PREACHING

•

The Pulpit at the Center

William H. Willimon

Abingdon Preacher's Library

William D. Thompson, Editor

ABINGDON

Nashville

INTEGRATIVE PREACHING: THE PULPIT AT THE CENTER

Copyright © 1981 by Abingdon

Library of Congress Cataloging in Publication Data
WILLIMON, WILLIAM H.
  Integrative preaching.
  (Abingdon preacher's library)
  Bibliography: p.
  Includes index.
  1. Preaching. I. Title.
  BV4211.2.W5   1981   251   80-39628
                  ISBN 0-687-19129-7

MANUFACTURED BY THE PARTHENON PRESS AT
NASHVILLE, TENNESSEE, UNITED STATES OF AMERICA

To the people
of Northside United Methodist Church,
who permit me to preach
on Sunday so that they may preach
the rest of the week.

EDITOR'S FOREWORD

Preaching has captured the attention of increasingly large segments of the American public. Lay parish committees seeking pastoral leadership consistently rank preaching as the most desirable pastoral skill. Seminary courses and clergy conferences on preaching attract participants in larger numbers than ever. Millions of viewers watch television preachers every week.

What is *good* preaching? is the question of both those who hear it and those who do it. Hearers answer that question instinctively, tuning in the preacher who meets their needs, whether in the pulpit of the neighborhood church or on a broadcast. Preachers need to answer more intentionally.

Time was that a good thick book on preaching would do it, or a miscellaneous smattering of thin ones. The time now seems ripe for a different kind of resource—a carefully conceived, tightly edited series of books whose scope covers the homiletical spectrum and whose individual volumes reveal the latest and best thinking about each specialty within the field of preaching. The volumes in the Abingdon Preacher's Library enable the preacher to understand preaching in its historical setting; to examine its biblical and theological underpinnings; to explore its spiritual, relational, and liturgical dimensions; and to develop insights into its craftsmanship.

Designed primarily for use in the seminary classroom, this series will also serve the practicing preacher whose background in homiletics is spotty or out-of-date, or whose preaching needs strengthening in some specific area.

William D. Thompson
Eastern Baptist Theological Seminary
Philadelphia, Pennsylvania

CONTENTS

INTRODUCTION

In former days—at least if you were a Baptist, Methodist, Presbyterian, or other free-church Christian—no one had any doubt where preaching was located. Everyone knew that preaching was at the center.

In the church where I grew up, the architecture itself depicted the centrality of preaching. As we entered the auditorium, our eyes were immediately led toward the front, to the central pulpit, high and prominent, placed above everything else in the room. Behind the pulpit are the choir and the big gold pipes of the organ—obviously there to back up the preacher's performance. Next to the pulpit was the large chair. There the preacher sat, deep in thought throughout the hymns, prayers, and readings—the preliminaries, as we sometimes referred to these prior acts of worship—until his time came. Surrounding the pulpit, in close, tiered, half-circled rows of pews, sat the congregation, clustered around "the sacred desk" to hear the word of God.

And when the preacher finally stepped up to that pulpit to preach, both pastor and congregation considered that moment the most important time in their week. The pastor was mostly a person who preached. The congregation was mostly a group who listened.

Today many criticize what I have somewhat nostalgically described. In the past few decades, a score of critics have attacked this architectural arrangement and the view of ministry it represents. The neglect of the sacraments in worship, the clerical dominance of the service, the passive participation of the congregation, the clergy-choir performance, and the promotion of homiletical vanity and pomposity were often the bad fruit of this conception of preaching. The centrality of the pulpit became totalitarian, until all ministry, all possibilities for lay participation, and all other functions of ministry were consumed by preaching.

We now know that it is theologically, historically, biblically, and practically unwise to elevate preaching at the expense of other historic elements in worship and other necessary pastoral functions. Some of our former confidence in the ability of preaching to teach, train, convert, win, and change people has been shaken by recent research, which, more often than not, shows all the things preaching cannot do rather than what it can do. For many modern clergy the preaching office seems dull, traditionalist, authoritarian, or a waste of precious pastoral time. Counseling, administration, community work, or social activism have pushed preaching to the periphery of a pastor's week. A few years ago when the new pastor of Christ Church (United Methodist) in Manhattan removed the pulpit altogether and did his preaching from behind the communion table, many of us thought his action signaled the death of the centrality of preaching in Protestantism.

So what is this—another dated book trying to resuscitate preaching and argue, all evidence to the contrary, for its importance? Or if this book cannot convince a new generation of preachers that preaching is crucial, it can perhaps at least make some feel guilty that they are investing less in their preaching than they should?

I hope this book is more helpful.

In my last parish I played a game with my pastor-parish relations committee that reminded me of something we preachers are constantly forgetting: the continued centrality of preaching. I took a set of 3" x 5" notecards and wrote one pastoral activity on each card. I then arranged the cards in the order of priority for me. At that time my church was beset by financial problems, lack of youth participation, and no growth in membership. Therefore my first four pastoral priorities were visitation of prospective members, visitation of nonactive members, youth ministry, and then preaching. At the next meeting of the pastor-parish relations committee I gave the cards to the members and asked them to arrange the cards in order of their highest priorities for my commitment of time. To my surprise their ranking went something like this: preaching, teaching, visitation of prospective members, and so on.

When I asked why they rated the responsibilities in this order, their responses indicated that they continued to see preaching as the primary pastoral activity, the one from which all other pastoral leadership flows. They could think of no more appropriate way to attract new members, no better way to energize inactive members, no better way to care for our youth than through good preaching. Of course their ranking still did not tell me what their idea of "good" preaching was. Nevertheless, it did remind me that in spite of all the good, understandable, modern reasons why preaching should not be at the center of a modern church's life, it still is at the center —at least in many people's minds.

My committee's responses have been confirmed by every other survey I have seen—among Protestant congregations—that asks laity to rate the importance of various pastoral functions. If my memory serves me correctly, most of the books that declared the death of preaching in the past two decades were written by *preachers!* In the first chapter I shall reflect upon some of the possible theological and psychological reasons why preaching is not central in many pastors' minds. But now, I simply want to say that preaching *is* at the center of the pastoral task, whether a preacher finds that understandable or not, whether or not the preacher finds satisfaction in preaching.

Preaching continues to be central in congregational life for two main reasons:

1. *Preaching is at the center of pastoral functions for practical reasons.* In preaching, pastors are seen and heard by more parishioners and are present in a more intentional, directed, visible, and purposeful way for an extended period of time than in any other pastoral situation. Pastors could spend many weeks of exhausting house-to-house visitation and not have as great an opportunity to guide and sustain their people as is afforded in the sermon. Any pastors who let other pastoral tasks overwhelm the preaching task are simply not using their time well.

Another practical reason why preaching is central is that in most churches—at least in most Protestant churches—people value preaching, want good preaching, and expect their pastors to be preachers. If our theology of the ordained ministry affirms (as we Protestants have traditionally affirmed and as ecumenical studies in ordination are now affirming) that the ordained ministry arises out of and is given meaning by the ministry of all Christians, then we must take with great seriousness what the people expect and ask of their ordained representatives. Whether pastors find preaching personally fulfilling or easy makes little difference. Personal fulfillment is not the point of the ordained ministry. The point is service, enablement, and equipment of the ministry of all Christians. Preaching is practically important because Christians continue to regard it as central to their needs as Christians.

2. *Preaching is at the center of pastoral functions for theological reasons.* Other books in this Abingdon Preacher's Library deal with the theological, biblical, and liturgical bases of preaching. This book is mostly concerned with the practical,

pastoral fruits of preaching in the congregation. But we ought to say here that preaching is central to the church's life for theological reasons that are as valid now as ever. The word of God is not something encased in our tradition. It must be spoken and it must be spoken in our time and place by men and women who are called into the service of that word. There is no church where the Name is not named, the story is not told, the word is not spoken.

Our Lord himself came to preach, and he sent out others to say what they had seen and heard. Faith never occurs in a vacuum, in silence. So although preaching is not the only way the church testifies to what she has seen and heard, it has always been the major way she has testified. In the biblical faith we have received, preaching is at the center.

ABOUT THIS BOOK

This book does not presume to break new ground. My survey of homiletical literature has convinced me that most of what we say about preaching has been said before. Therefore I will probably be saying things you have heard before. But I remind you that we preachers repeat ourselves, not only because we know nothing new to say but also because some things need to be said again within different contexts to meet changing needs.

Nor could I in a book of this limited length and scope, hope to show all the various ways preaching is central for pastoral work and the church's life.

What I do hope to show is that preaching has an inherently integrative quality. It both contributes to and receives strength from other areas of ministry. Toward this centering activity of the church, the church's hopes, disappointments, questions, visions, and needs move in hope of interpretation, inspiration, and liberation. From this centering activity the church's mission, edification, pastoral care, and witness arise.

In one sense most of my fellow pastors already know and have experienced in their own ministry the integrative qualities of preaching that I reflect upon in this book. So the goal of this book is to raise consciousness of and increase sensitivity to integrative preaching on the part of pastors so that they may better claim and enrich the integrative preaching that is already occurring within their congregations.

My thanks to my students at Duke Divinity School, to my secretary, Mrs. Clinton Chappell, to my ministerial colleagues, especially Dr. Richard Lischer at Duke and the ministers of the Greenville District of The United Methodist Church, and to the people of Northside United Methodist Church, who enriched this book through their shared experiences of integrative preaching and who enriched me simply by being the people they are.

Marion Hatchett, who teaches at the University of the South, tells of overhearing a conversation between two women about their former pastor. One woman said, "I realize that Joe was not a good preacher. But he was a good pastor. He was a wonderful pastor to me when I went through my difficult times."

The other woman replied, "I couldn't disagree with you more. I think Joe was a poor pastor. I never had a death in my family while he was here, never had serious illness or difficulty. But we attended church every Sunday, and it was obvious that Joe did not care enough about this congregation to prepare his sermons carefully and speak to us. I was there every Sunday, and he was never a good pastor for me."

Amid all the responsibilities pastors are required to carry out in our modern world, I hope we can remember the conversation of those two Christians. It should remind us that the place of the pulpit—not so much architecturally as theologically and pastorally—in the church of the past, the present, and the foreseeable future is at the center.

Northside Church
Pentecost, 1980

I. THE PASTOR AS PREACHER

Recently I asked a number of rural North Carolina congregations to define good preaching. The first thing I noted in these lay persons' responses was that most of them defined it by naming good preachers. They seemed to be unable to separate the preacher from the preaching. When they listed characteristics of good sermons, they listed personality traits such as warmth, honesty, friendliness, excitement. Therefore when many lay persons think of good preaching, they associate it with a good preacher.

The second thing I noted was that when they named the great preachers of our day, they invariably mentioned one of the new media preachers, one of the stars of the radio or television pulpit: Roberts, Graham, or Schuller. Granted a myriad of questionable reasons why someone might be attracted to the preaching of these stars—their showmanship, glamour, or simplistic theology—lay respondents listed one characteristic of their preaching over and over again: *they preach as if they were preaching to individual listeners and their problems.*

Although I do not mean to elevate these television preachers as examples of good Christian preaching, those of us who preach Sunday after Sunday within a congregation need to be reminded from time to time that preaching never occurs in a vacuum. All truth that comes from the pulpit is, in Phillips Brooks's often quoted phrase, "truth through personality." It is also truth touching the needs of persons.

THE WORD IN CONTEXT

A generation ago Harry Emerson Fosdick discovered as a young preacher that the place to begin a sermon was

> with the real problems of the people. That was a sermon's specialty, which made it a sermon, not an essay or a lecture. Every sermon should have for its main business the head-on constructive meeting of some problem which was puzzling minds, burdening consciences, distracting lives, and no sermon which so met a real human difficulty, with light to throw on it and help to win a victory over it, could possibily be futile.[1]

Fosdick's "life-situation preaching" had certain weaknesses: its use of the Bible as secondary appendage to a sermon taking its cue from life rather than from the text, its problem-solving approach, and so on. Because of Fosdick's personal love for and knowledge of the Bible, he was usually able to keep his sermons tied to the text, but a succeeding generation of topical and life-situation preachers who copied him was not so successful. Fosdick was revolting against a sterile kind of biblical preaching that was largely irrelevant to the emerging twentieth-century mind.

Unlike Fosdick, the disciples of Barth and the biblical theology movement tended to view preaching in an almost magical sense, as if mere repetition of specifically biblical terms and mere accurate explication of biblical texts were efficacious for a person's salvation through preaching. They minimized the preacher's role as communicator, apologete, and problem solver. As Barth said, "Preaching is not intended to be simply a clearer and more adequate explanation of life than can be arrived at by other means. . . . The congregation is waiting for the meaning of life to be illumined by the light of God."[2] God's Word was to be confessed by the preacher, confessed in accuracy and humility—and that was enough.

Although this approach to preaching was a helpful corrective to the human-centered, life-situation, and topical preaching of liberal Protestantism, it was most unbiblical in its rather priestly and mystical view of the word in Scripture and preaching. The Bible is a historically situated and contextualized book, and the revelation in it was neither given nor received within a vacuum. Revelation arises out of and is brought to specific people in specific places at specific times. Part of the difficult task of biblical exegesis is to determine the shape of this specific context. Recent canonical criticism reminds us that not only does the revelation of the Bible arise out of specific historical contexts but also that the texts were subsequently arranged and appropriated by Israel and the church to meet the changing and emerging contexts of the people of God in other times and places.

The exegetical and hermeneutical skills a preacher acquires are, in great part, skills in uncovering and rediscovering the originating and continuing intepretative context for the text. So in one sense, all preaching from the Bible is "life-situation" preaching—not only preaching to the life-situation of the twentieth century but also preaching out of the life-situation of the centuries before us when God spoke to the life-situation of God's people then. To deny or overlook that context, within the text or within the church today, is to be most unbiblical in overlooking the incarnational, historically contextualized nature of Scripture.

Preaching is the pastoral activity that unites these two life-situation contexts in such a way that today's hearers of the word hear the ancient word as God's Word for them. This cannot be done without skillful exegetical listening to the scriptural text, nor can it be done without skillful pastoral listening to the congregational context. This is why not only the most relevant preaching but also the most biblical preaching must be *pastoral* preaching, arising out of the intimate pastoral interaction between pastor and people within the congregation.

A WARNING

But now a warning must be sounded. Granted, the life-situation of the text must be related to the life-situation of the people who now stand before this text in the sermon. Granted that good preaching must reflect the person of the pastor attempting to communicate the truth of the gospel to the needs of persons in the congregation. But are there not pitfalls along this path of pastoral preaching?

At its best, pastoral preaching is relevant, pointed, biblical, and challenging. Whenever the word hits home, convicts us, touches us, encourages us, prods us where we live, these are moments for which Christian congregations and preachers live. But at its worst, topical preaching is trivial, culture and time bound to current clichés and preoccupations, moralistic, and petty. "Ten Steps to a Happy Marriage," "How Should We Vote in the Next Schoolboard Election?" "Suggestions for Inspirational Summer Reading," are actual sermon topics I have heard—and I have even preached some of them!

We humans are always under the temptation, in our dialogue with the biblical text, to take ourselves more seriously than the text, to elevate our problems or concerns over whatever concerns the text may be addressing. When this happens, we cease to listen to the text and start to speak to it instead. Dialogue becomes monologue, with the preacher and congregation doing all the talking. Exegesis becomes eisegesis. Hermeneutic becomes polemic. The text becomes a pretext for talking about what we wanted to say before we looked at the text, and saying what we want to say in spite of the text. This is less than true Christian preaching.

I think we Americans are especially attracted to this kind of topical, human-centered and -initiated preaching. We are a pragmatic, goal-oriented, problem-solving people. We want a religion that works, that offers some active, immediate result and payoff in the sermon. And so utilitarianism is the greatest homiletical danger we face.

Preaching that falls under the spell of utilitarianism, that seeks some quick, useful, and easy payoff, that uses the sermon for some purpose other than the proclamation of the truth of the gospel—even such noble purposes as pastoral care, teaching, edification, or counseling—is preaching that is being used and is thereby being abused.

I disagree with Fosdick that the place to begin a sermon is "with the real problems of the people." Preachers who begin with people's needs rarely offer more than people's solutions to people's problems, and there is nothing specifically Christian or divine or ultimately significant about that. The place to *begin* is with the Word, with the Bible, with the tradition and Scripture of the church. A sermon is not made a Christian sermon simply by addressing the needs of the people. Only a sermon that arises out of the standpoint of the biblical testimony can be Christian. Only by beginning there can the sermon be specifically and truly Christian.

In the pulpit we first speak of God's deeds rather than humanity's needs. Without God's ceaseless activity and striving after us, we know neither our true needs nor our true selves. The gospel is not a set of propositions to be mastered and agreed with. The gospel *is* a proclamation that God, in Jesus Christ, has acted and continues to act to save the same humanity that, time and again, has demonstrated it cannot save itself. The gospel is not a set of principles that, if we follow them, will lead to a better life.

The gospel *is* a proclamation that we save our life only by losing it in Christ, that we find the promised abundant life only by way of the cross.

Preaching—Christian preaching—compels only when a compelling message grasps the preacher. When a message grasps the messenger, the sermon lives and breathes and soars. Otherwise the sermon quickly degenerates into a set of moral platitudes or a painfully amateurish attempt at group therapy—both of which may sometimes be moderately helpful but never ultimately, decisively helpful to the listeners.

The other day a colleague who had been working with a difficult translation problem in an ancient manuscript burst into my office and recounted loudly and excitedly what he had just discovered. He had run all the way down the hall and banged on my door to tell me. So if you hear something important—really important—you will find a way to share it. You will get the attention of your hearers when you yourself hear something worth telling, and your listeners will listen because we all are interested in any message that so excites the messenger. This, I think, is where truly *Christian* preaching begins.

In this matter of topical preaching I like the distinction Ronald Sleeth makes between the *content* and the *form* of preaching. Sleeth says that most topical preaching goes astray when the preacher makes the life-situation—the topical human need—the specific content of the sermon rather than the form. So the preacher sets out, for example, to speak to the need of human suffering. The preacher states the need, analyzes the reasons for suffering, and gives some advice for living with or overcoming suffering. Even when the preacher uses biblical materials along the way to arrive at a solution of the problem, the approach he or she uses is invariably intellectual, analytical, psychological—never formed or closely guided by the Bible. "Such a treatment may be very helpful, but in the final analysis it is good advice, not good news."[3] The sermon must be kerygmatic before it is didactic or therapeutic.

Sleeth says that the content and substance of the sermon must always be, not simply our questions, our needs, our situation, but the witness of the Bible. Our questions, needs, and situation may, however, be used to construct a *form* for the sermon, an approach in the sermon that can relate the content of Scripture to the needs of the hearers.

Edmund Steimle begins one of his memorable "Protestant Hour" sermons this way:

> What happens when a person dies? Is this life all there is? Death is easier to accept when it comes to an older person late in life. But what about when a child dies in a ditch at My Lai, life snuffed out before it has a chance to live? What about that child's death? Is that all there is?

Then Steimle reads two biblical texts, one from Job, the other from Thessalonians, to tell us what the *Bible* indicates about life after death.

Admittedly, no person communicates with another person without some purpose, some useful end, in mind. Any good preacher, as the young Fosdick learned, sets out to confront a specific life-situation or need with the truth of the gospel. But this does not necessitate using the gospel in a quasitherapeutic attempt to do something nice for people. As we said above, when a sermon begins that way, it derails before it gets started.

Rather, to speak of the pastoral dimension of preaching, the inherently integrative quality of the preaching event, is to remind ourselves that while the sermon is being kerygmatic it is also frequently being didactic and therapeutic. While we are proclaiming the gospel, in faithfulness and humility before the sacred text, we are also offering pastoral care to the people who stand before the text. While we are preaching, other things are happening to our congregations and to us as a by-product of our preaching. This book affirms the biblical text as the place to begin a sermon, the place from which the preacher's metaphors, concepts, and truth must be derived. Yet it also seeks to show that before the preaching event is finished, significant counseling, edification of the community, teaching, social action, and worship often will have taken place for both the pastor and the people.

THE PASTORAL CONTEXT

The stars of the radio and television pulpit may be entertaining, and their sermons at times may be helpful, engaging, even biblical. But their preaching will never achieve the depth, the specificity, and the power of great Christian preaching—because they all attempt to be preachers without being pastors. The gathered congregation is the context for great Christian preaching, not simply as a source for homiletical illustration, nor simply as a target for the sermons. The gathered congregation is the setting because the Bible is the church's book. It was written by, arose out of, and speaks specifically to the gathered people of God. Only the preacher who has first been pastor can know and speak to this people.

The difficulty of great biblical preaching is the difficulty of being in two places at once—the pulpit *and* the pew. To preach "biblically"—in the sense of engaging the living Word of God with the living people of God—one must be not only the biblical scholar in the study but also the pastor present in the living room, hospital room, kitchen, front porch, office, and on the assembly line.

"Get inside the mind of your hearers," Spurgeon told the preachers of his day. But you cannot get into their minds without getting into their homes, schools, offices, and factories, or into their unemployment lines, prison cells, and nursing homes. I have never been fond of pastoral visitation—it takes time, money, energy. Particularly difficult is placing myself at the disposal of my parishioners, coming to them rather than their coming to me, meeting them on their own turf rather than on mine. And yet that same difficulty is at the heart of good preaching: the difficulty of *listening*. Hearing—the kind of deep, sensitive, vulnerable, intimate hearing that preaching requires—arises out of humble, patient, continuous listening. A congregation tends to listen to someone who has first listened.

Fred Craddock advocates what he calls the "inductive method of preaching." His method calls for a somewhat unorthodox approach to our use of the Bible in preaching and our general method of sermon preparation and construction, for it advocates constant immersion in the day-to-day, concrete aspects of human life in order to allow the gospel to speak to human life. "Impression is necessary for expression," says Craddock:

> When the pastor writes a sermon, an empathetic imagination sees again those concrete experiences with his people which called upon all his resources, drove him to the Bible and back again, and even now hang as vivid pictures in his mind. When a pastor preaches, he doesn't sell patent medicine; he writes prescriptions. Others may hurl epithets at the "wealthy" but the pastor knows a lonely and guilt-ridden man confused by the Bible's debate with itself over prosperity: Is prosperity a sign of God's favor or disfavor? Others may display knowledge of "poverty programs" but the pastor knows what a bitter thing it is to be somebody's Christmas project. He sees a boy resisting his mother's insistence that he wear the nice sweater that came in the charity basket. He can see the boy wear it until out of Mother's sight, but not at school out of fear that he may meet the original owner on the playground. There are conditions worse than being cold. Others may discuss "the problem of geriatrics" but the pastor has just come from the local rest home and he still sees worn checkerboards, faded bouquets, large print King James Bibles, stainless steel trays, and dim eyes staring at an empty parking lot reserved for visitors. . . . Some ministers have conducted them-

selves on the principle that too much involvement in the lives of the parishioners constitutes an overexposure which weakens the force of their preaching. In other words, distance is essential to authority. In terms of one traditional view of the ministry, this observation is correct, but the inductive method cannot live with that image. In the inductive method it is essential that the minister really be a member of the congregation he serves.[4]

So preaching is no mere mechanical process or technique. On the contrary it is communication of the innermost being of a person in relationship with other persons—"truth through personality," as Brooks first noted. The pastoral relationship is therefore not merely helpful to preaching, it is essential. Even Barth, who laid such stress upon the objectivity of the Word, recognized the essentially relational nature of preaching:

> The preacher will live the life of his congregation, placing himself on their level. He does not have to be the wise man of the people, the village diviner who lays bare the innermost thoughts of men's hearts, but the question of what their innermost thoughts really are is always in his mind.[5]

Many sermons never reach their targets because they are not aimed. They are preached by preachers who, although they may be good pastors, keep their homiletical purposes and their pastoral insights in separate compartments. The connection between the two ministerial functions is coincidental rather than intentional: implicit, haphazard.

But the average local pastor who is present in the midst of the humdrum, day-to-day life of the people of God, who has personally had his or her nose rubbed in the nitty-gritty of their visions and fears, their dreams and dashed hopes, preaches from the heart and life of the congregation. Such a pastor is better prepared to preach than any of the polished television pulpit stars with their make-up and technical advisers or, for that matter the "princes of the pulpit" who perform before congregations of more than two thousand members each Sunday while staffs of associates and paid church visitors relieve them of daily pastoral chores so that they can prepare for next Sunday's performance.[6]

Our most important—indeed, imperative—task, therefore, is to look for ways to make the pastoral relationship a more integral and intentional part of our preaching. After the commentaries have been consulted, after the preacher has humbly and expectantly studied the Scripture for a given Sunday, then the preacher must, in the words of my late colleague, Jim Cleland, "paint the Word with local colour":

> Now the minister must clear his desk of the accumulated Bibles and commentaries, and in his mind's eye visualize his congregation to whose advantage he is going to expound this Word. What do they look like? What are they busy at in the World? What kind of folk make up his flock? It is not enough to see them as plumbers and store clerks and income tax collectors; as stenographers and housewives and old maids; as professors, firemen and Pullman porters. He must picture them more individually. There is a waitress who, poor soul, chronically suffers from hay fever, and a night watchman who understandably goes to sleep during the sermon. There is a widow and her three neatly dressed children who never miss the eleven o'clock service. . . . There is a college boy who is present during the vacations, but only because he is under the discipline of home. It is a motley company of men and women who traffic and market in the streets of the World, who find much of their amusement and recreation there, who are renters of houses and builders of homes, and who come to church—sometimes, often, regularly. Them he must see. He must smile at them, and not to them, and talk with them as he mulls over his sermon. He must know them, really know them. That is why pastoral visitation is a *sine qua non* of helpful preaching.[7]

After my first six months in my last congregation, I sat down one afternoon and listed all the things I had learned about my

people since I had been there, all the conclusions I had drawn
about them that must be relevant for my preaching:

1. They are theological creatures who, though they may not
   speak in theological categories, are trying to make sense
   out of life and are grateful for help in doing so.
2. They already know, down deep, most of their real
   problems and now need help, not more diagnosis.
3. Their essential condition is one of powerlessness, or at
   least what feels like powerlessness; they are more the
   victims of life than the villians. Most of the things they do
   not like about themselves, most of the things they would
   like to change, they will not be able to change.
4. They respond more to an appeal to their creativity than to
   an appeal to their fear.
5. They value stability in the midst of the changes life is
   imposing upon them. If they cannot achieve stability, if
   they cannot feel some underlying order and sense to it all,
   they will simply cling to the status quo.
6. They must have some vision of their future in order to live
   in the present. If they cannot perceive a reliable vision,
   they will grasp false hopes or else fall into cynicism and
   despair.
7. They think concretely and in pictures. They do not read
   much. Therefore, they think by means of stories and
   images.

Of course my list is not exhaustive. These are only my
personal pastoral observations. But the process of systematic,
intentional listening—listening as a prelude to preaching—is
essential for preaching.

Abstraction, generalization, and universalization are, as
Kierkegaard noted, the persistent enemies of the gospel—the
gospel whose particularity is its chief scandal. Good preaching

communicates the gospel with scandalous particularity so that it hits home to people in such a way that they have little doubt that the truth is addressed to *this* people, living in *this* place, at *this* time. Only one who knows the particulars of this people can proclaim the gospel in its particularity. That is why Kierkegaard said that humility is the greatest virtue for the religious speaker: it is the prerequisite for the gospel. "First of all take pains to find him where he is and begin there," says Kierkegaard.[8] When the one who knows addresses the Word to those who are known, they will know that the Word is being spoken to them, in their particularity, demanding a particular response from them.

In seminary I teach courses in preaching or worship. I would at times like to be able to assure these future preachers that the authority for their preaching comes solely from ecclesiastical endorsement through ordination, or from accurate biblical exegesis and hermeneutics through their conscientious application of those skills, or from good sermon construction and delivery by following my methods. Fledgling preachers might find it reassuring to believe that technique or external authorization convey authority.

But in all honesty I am forced to admit that a great part of a preacher's authority is *earned*. We do bring with us the authority of the church's tradition, the power of the Scriptures, the people's willingness to give us the benefit of the doubt. But authority also arises out of the day-to-day pastoral work that we do. The congregation believes that ultimately only the one who has faithfully exercised the right to listen has the right to speak.

From time to time I have heard homileticians speak of the need for personal "presence" in preaching, the need for a person honestly to share his or her innermost personality and feelings in a sermon. This presence is important. But like it or not, for most congregations the most important "presence" is the pastor's presence at bedsides, in committee meetings, on youth retreats, during marital difficulties. The listening and dialogue in such presence gives the preacher the authority to preach. Perhaps more accurately, such presence provides the context whereby the Word can be spoken with the particularity that is, in itself, its own authority.

This insight came to me during the years when I was out of the parish and teaching in a seminary. During that time I did nearly as much preaching as when I was in the pastorate. But I felt the constant frustration of the visiting-fireman syndrome: the visiting pulpit star blows into town, spreads a little warmth, and delivers a series of stirring but often irrelevant platitudes. The visiting preacher is admired by the people for his skill or else dismissed by them for his foreignness. In either case he is not really *heard*. Such preaching must rely for its authority—as does that of TV pulpit preachers—on good looks, or charisma, or dazzling intellect, or a large background choir. This is less than Christian preaching.

In one of my former pastorates, I had many visitors on Sundays during the summer months because we were in a resort area. On one Sunday one of the lectionary texts was Paul's comments on marriage in Ephesians. In reflecting upon Paul's view, which I characterized as mutual submission, I tried to speak honestly of my own frustrations and disappointments over the marital difficulties our own congregation had been experiencing. At the end of the service, after most persons had left the sanctuary, one tourist, stayed behind.

He thanked me for the sermon and said he had found it particularly helpful because of what he termed its honesty and forthrightness.

"There's only one thing I can't understand," he said. "Surely someone must have felt very uncomfortable during your sermons. I would think some might even have been angry. How is it that they let you preach like this Sunday after Sunday?"

"You overlook one thing," I said. "I am not only their preacher, I'm their pastor. They know that when they have marital problems, I'm the first one there to offer help and support. They know that the one who speaks these difficult words of judgment from the Bible is also the one who tries to be compassionate and understanding when they can't fulfill these demands in their own marriages. Furthermore, they know me and my own marriage, and so they know these are the words of a fellow struggler. I preach these things not only because they're in the Bible and I have an obligation to preach them but also because they're addressed to me and my people and I have the right to preach them."

Bold, pointed, biblical preaching always springs from the singular authority of a pastoral context.

This pastoral context for preaching is of course not only an integral part of a sermon's creation but also a part of the response. A sermon is a personal, relational process, not a product. It is a multidimensional, long term event, not an object. Obviously, printed sermons read out of their congregational context are never as fully effective as the real thing, because a sermon cannot be objectified, isolated, or taken out of the context of the community within which it was prepared, delivered, and responded to.

Sermon preparation is not simply a matter of the pastor's preparatory listening, reading, meditation, prayer, and writing. Preparing a sermon also involves, in all sorts of subtle ways, preparing a congregation for the sermon. The personal relationship, the goals of the congregation, the achievements and disappointments for its ministry and outreach, and the congregational perception of the pastor all contribute to congregational receptivity and response.

We can prepare a congregation for a sermon through presermon study and/or discussion groups, either with the pastor or among the laity themselves. Research has shown that such presermon groups not only contribute to the preacher's sermon preparation but also make the laity more receptive and more skillful listeners. When church Bible-study groups or church school classes study the appointed scripture lessons before the day the lessons are to be preached, members come to church already primed for the sermon. And when daily devotional materials such as The Upper Room *Disciplines*, are keyed to the lectionary, they provide yet another way of congregational sermon preparation and response.

A presermon phone call or visit to selected members of the congregation also helps people integrate their lives into the sermon and see that their preacher is preaching with pastoral care. A remark such as "I hope you're going to be at church next Sunday, because I'm going to be preaching on the need for forgiveness," or "After our conversation last week, I thought you might find the sermon helpful," can be the beginning of a significant encounter between someone and the Word.

Within the sermon itself the preacher can use certain phrases to help listeners see the relationship between their congregational questions and needs and the scripture: "The other night in the board meeting, I got to thinking. . . ." or, "This has been a tough week for our church—the closing of the town's biggest employer, the death of one of our beloved members. In times like these we wonder what . . ." or "I know from recent conversation that many of you are worried about the future. Today's gospel lesson speaks to those of us who . . ."

But in the context of the congregation, no sermon should end when the preacher is finished speaking. It does not have to be tied up, neat and finished, after three points and a poem. Indeed the sermon may well be the beginning of the kind of dialogue out of which proclamation arises. When people file out the front door on their way home after church and say to the preacher "I didn't like what you said today. That's not what I've always believed. . . ," or "I was a bit confused by your sermon. I don't understand why . . . " they are not necessarily telling the preacher that he has failed to communicate. Indeed, such responses to the sermon may indicate that real communication has just begun. Then the preacher's responsibility is to provide an occasion whereby the process can continue.

The next Sunday's sermon is one place for follow-up. But a personal and individualized setting might be more appropriate. "Let's get together for lunch tomorrow and talk about it," or, "You seem troubled by what I said. When can we talk more about the sermon?" would be ways for the preacher to continue the process of proclamation through pastoral contact. At our church, "Lemonade and conversation" is offered in the church parlor for thirty minutes after the Sunday service for those who want to discuss the sermon.

No sermon begins when the Bible is opened and the day's text is read. Nor does the sermon end when the preacher sits down and the last hymn is sung. Every sermon is a long, continuous process of communication and relationship that must be pastoral if it is to be effective.

A CONCLUDING OBSERVATION ON
PASTORS WHO ARE NOT PREACHERS

After an opening word on the television pulpit stars who attempt to be preachers without being pastors, I end with a word on pastors who do not want to be preachers.

We may at last have grown out of the sixties' put-down of preaching. Recent works in communications theory, biblical studies, and pastoral theology—many of them in this Abingdon Preacher's Library—have restored the importance of preaching for the church.

But many congregations continue to express bafflement that their pastors apparently find preaching unworthy of their greatest effort. As Lee Keck notes in his fine book on biblical preaching,

preaching has lost its centrality in most main-line white Protestant churches, although it has never lost its place in black Protestantism and is being rediscovered in the Catholic Church. The white Protestant pastor who still devotes a major block of his time preparing sermons—especially scholarly or biblical ones—has been on the endangered species list for a long time. Today it is administration that gets the lion's share of one's energy. What is left is apportioned to counseling and routine pastoral care, "board sitting" on community agencies; sundry matters have displaced Sunday matters. The proliferation of tasks has squeezed virtually to the vanishing point blocks of time free from interruption, time essential for sermon preparation and especially for long-range reading and reflection.[9]

"He's not much of a preacher," congregations sometimes say, "but he is a wonderful pastor"—the same way we used to speak, somewhat cruelly, about a disappointing date in high school: "She's not good looking, but she is a great conversationalist." Of course anyone would know that we preferred good looks! The same goes for congregations who attempt to excuse poor preaching.

I hope that by the end of this chapter you agree there can be no "good preacher" who is not also a good pastor. The converse is also true: there are no good pastors who are not good preachers.

For a minister to allow administrative work, counseling, study, visitation, teaching, or any other worthy pastoral function to crowd out preaching is wrong. In preaching the pastor makes explicit what is often implicit in most pastoral encounters: the specific claims of the gospel. In preaching, the Name is named, the story is told, and the truth is made explicit and public. If pastoral work is allowed to proceed as if being a pastor means simply doing good things for people, or solving people's problems, or oiling organizational machinery, or directing a program of activities, or making pleasant conversation with shut-ins and prospective members, then the whole point, the distinctive, identifying characteristic of Christian ministry, is missed.

I agree with Ronald Sleeth that many pastors today question the value of preaching—its ineffectiveness in communication or its authoritarian theological tendencies—when their real problem with preaching is with their own being rather than with any inherent weaknesses in preaching.[10] Preaching is threatening because it reveals, as do few other pastoral activities, the innermost parts of who are and how we personally stand in relation to this gospel we are called to proclaim. It is the very explicitness, the unveiling, the public exposure of preaching, that is its power and its threat.

Many preachers devalue preaching, not because it is irrelevant but because it is difficult. As Moses found out when he stood before the burning bush, it is hard to speak and listen to God. And as Moses found out when he stood before Pharaoh or the children of Israel, it is equally hard to speak to people about God. Such is the burden of preaching. And so the Cure says in Georges Bernanos's *Diary of a Country Priest*, "To stand before one's peers and the Eternal God is not the easiest of vocations."

In succeeding chapters I hope to show how preaching integrates selected pastoral activities into the life of the church by enabling the relationships of these activities to the gospel to become explicit and intentional. In preaching the pastor also shows, in an explicit and public way, that whatever the pastor does within the congregation in an official capacity he or she does as one who is under orders to preach the gospel. When the relationship between the preaching task and the other pastoral functions is seen, then all the other functions are more likely to become occasions for proclamation and witness to the gospel.

A friend of mine who is a full-time licensed pastoral counselor has chosen to have his office within a local church. Part of his agreement with the church is that he is to preach at least one Sunday a month in that church. He insists on preaching because, in his words, "Preaching helps me identify who I am as a truly pastoral counselor, and it helps the congregation set my work in the communal context of God's ultimate judgment and grace which is witnessed to by this congregation." Preaching continually reminds pastors who they are and under whose mandate they serve.

The greatest temptation of us modern preachers, I think, is, not the temptation to say too much, but the temptation to say too little. Silence is our great tempter. It is easier for us to let the truth go unspoken, to allow the claims of the gospel to remain implicit, to busy ourselves with doing many things rather than undertaking and allowing ourselves to be undertaken by the task of speaking the truth in love.

Many of us would like to be preachers without being pastors—delivering inspiring moral platitudes, speaking of the eternal with a suitably dramatic flair, engrossing ourselves in high-sounding phrases and deep thoughts—without once speaking to our peers in the faith, without muddying ourselves in the mundane, without listening.

Others of us would like to be pastors without being preachers—doing good things for good people, devising the right therapies for our people's sicknesses, directing church activities, building bigger and better churches—without once being forced to speak the truth that hurts us and them, without once pointing beyond ourselves to the One who is greater than our plans and projects.

But we cannot be preacher without being pastor and vice versa. Our preaching must be integrative if it is to be heard. Our pastoral work must be an adjunct to the homiletical endeavor if it is to be Christian.

Silence is indeed always tempting. And so, fresh from last Wednesday's squabble at the administrative board meeting, the divorce hearing of two of his members, and an afternoon of talking with old Mrs. Jones, who is just lonely, the pastor mounts the pulpit to be their preacher. As he looks out on the congregation he sees, not consumers of his sermonic skill or an audience to be entertained, but rather his flock—those who have received his pastoral care and who now await his preaching. In the words of Frederick Buechner, he sees this:

> In the front pews the old ladies turn up their hearing aids, and a young lady slips her six-year-old a Life Saver and a Magic Marker. A college sophomore home for vacation who is there because he was dragged there, slumps forward with his chin in his hand. The vice-president of a bank who twice this week has seriously contemplated suicide places his hymnal in the rack. A pregnant girl feels the life stir inside her. A high-school math teacher, who for twenty years has managed to keep his homosexuality a secret for the most part even from himself, creases his order of service down the center with his thumbnail and tucks it under his knee. . . .

> The preacher pulls the little cord that turns on the lectern light and deals out his note cards like a riverboat gambler. The stakes have never been higher. Two minutes from now he may have lost his listeners completely to their own thoughts, but at this minute he has them in the palm of his hand. The silence in the shabby church is deafening because everybody is listening to it. . . . Everybody knows the kind of things he has told them before and not told them, but who knows what this time, out of the silence, he will tell them?[11]

II. THE PREACHER AS COUNSELOR

The person who enters the pulpit to proclaim the Word on Sundays is also the person who has entered the homes, the lives, the hopes and fears, of his or her parishioners Mondays through Saturdays. The pastor is not only a preacher, he or she is also a counselor, one who guides, sustains, reconciles, and heals[1] the people of God as they go about the task of living the faith. As I have argued elsewhere, pastoral care is not limited to acts of pastoral counseling.[2] It encompasses a broad array of pastoral acts of guiding, sustaining, reconciling, and healing that go beyond the currently popular one-to-one or group counseling sessions.

Even though pastoral care is a broad, multifaceted activity of the one who shepherds the flock, this chapter focuses on pastoral counseling in order to suggest some of the ways it aids the preaching task and vice versa. I define pastoral counseling as *a process of growth or an act of crisis intervention in which the pastor is understood by the participants as being the pastoral helper, listener, adviser and counselor.* The goal of such counseling is to enable the recipients of this act of pastoral care to cope with some crisis situation and/or to grow both in their self-understanding and in their own faith.

I agree with Fosdick and others that important preaching—biblical preaching in the deepest sense of the phrase—speaks to persons' needs. The Word is never simply interesting information, noble ideas, or historical data. The Word is personal, a Person confronting persons, incarnational, in the flesh.

This does not mean that the sermon must always concern itself with personal problems, conflicts, and crises, however.

To say that preaching speaks to persons' needs is to be reminded of the breadth and depth of human need. Human beings do not simply need help in making the right decisions in a specific personal crisis, they also need help in finding deeper meaning in life as a whole. Human beings not only need to be sustained through various life crises, they also need a vision of where their lives are leading, a hope that it is all ultimately worthwhile, a prod to be all that God has called them to be. As Don Browning reminds us throughout his book on the larger theological setting of pastoral care, such care occurs within a theological-ethical setting and must push beyond mere non-directive listening and mere empathetic support to help persons develop a moral-theological context in which to view their specific problems and their lives as a whole.[3]

In other words, perhaps one of the greatest weaknesses of our former practice of life-situation preaching was, not that it attempted to speak to human needs in the sermon, but that it had too narrow and too limited a concept of what human need is.

But now a warning must be sounded. Although we are preaching to persons' needs, we must in David Switzer's words, beware of viewing "the sanctuary as a large couch and the preacher as a stand-up shrink."[4] Preaching cannot be, as Fosdick once tried to make it, "counseling on a group scale." Nor is it accurate to say, as does Arthur Teikmanis, that "dynamic preaching is basically pastoral care in the context of worship."[5] As Switzer says, pastoral functions such as preaching and pastoral care may support each other, or be mutually enriching, or lead to occasions for other pastoral functions, but they must be kept distinct.

In the following chapters of this book we must avoid the temptation to make statements such as "Good preaching is really good Christian education, or good counseling, or good administration," and so on. All these pastoral activities are carried out by the same pastor; they all share some of the same pastoral motivations and goals. The same congregation is the recipient of the care they attempt to give. But they are not basically the same. We have all seen preaching that attempts to create the intimate, personal, subjective, nondirectional qualities that often make for good pastoral counseling—and the result is rarely good Christian preaching. On the other hand, we have all seen pastoral counseling sessions that degenerate into sermonettes—scolding, berating, and Bible-quoting harangues—and the result is rarely good Christian counseling.

As I think of preaching and counseling and what makes these two pastoral activities mutually enriching and yet separate and distinctive, I think of them this way: Preaching is a public, corporate, traditioned and traditional, proclamation-oriented pastoral function. Counseling tends to be more personal, private, one to one, problem oriented.

In preaching, the preacher bears the burden of explicating and proclaiming the faith of the church, not simply his or her own thoughts, opinions, or personal experiences about the faith. Preaching is therefore inherently concerned with tradition: the traditional story of the church, its orthodox witness, its historic affirmations, the testimony of the saints, the criticism and encouragement of the canon and church tradition for the church today. Preaching is concerned not only with relating the tradition of the church to today's needs—what I might call "traditioning" today's church—but it is also one of the church's traditional activities. The form of preaching—its style, content, and methods—is inherently traditional: one person standing before a group of persons and witnessing to the truth of the gospel. Although in recent years many have accused preaching of being too traditional in its form and methods, I believe most congregations find the traditional modes the most satisfactory, either because they work or because they provide a congregation much-needed continuity and rootage in the midst of contemporary change.

In counseling, pastors can focus in an immediate, specific, and very personal way on the individual's specific needs, fears, feelings, questions, doubts, and aspirations. For although these questions and problems may be, in fact should be, seen within the context of the whole sweep of the church's tradition and witness, the main value of counseling is intensely personal. When pastors do not hear what the individual is saying or, trying to say—and trying not to say—counseling is less than it should be. So although preaching provides the occasion for a public, corporate, traditional confrontation with the Word, counseling provides the occasion for a personal, subjective, specific, immediate confrontation with the Word.

HOW COUNSELING AIDS PREACHING

Pastoral counseling provides a primary occasion for parishioners to be with their preacher in significant, personal, intimate relationships that establish necessary rapport. Sometimes preachers say their counseling experiences help their preaching because they reveal important information about parishioners. True. But we must not forget that counseling also provides an opportunity for parishioners to learn important things about their preacher. In one-to-one or small-group counseling experiences, persons have an opportunity to relate to their preacher in a personal, individualized setting. In this setting they often experience the preacher as a fellow human being who cares, who wants to know about their personal needs and worries and who takes time not only for the church as a whole but also for them as individuals. They also see the preacher as a person willing to be vulnerable to their feelings, secrets, and ambivalent motives as well as someone willing to share some of his or her feelings with them. As Paul said of his own ministry, whether in his counseling ministry or preaching ministry we know not, "So, being affectionately desirous of you, we were ready to share with you *not only the gospel of God but also our own selves,* because you had become very dear to us." (1 Thessalonians 2:8, italics mine) In a counseling encounter, we can become fellow pilgrims, companions in the struggle to live the faith in our daily lives, brothers and sisters who stand both under the grace and the judgment of the gospel.

Moreover, personal one-to-one or small-group relationships that develop in our counseling help set our preaching in a deeper and more personal context then we can achieve in our more public leadership roles.

One pastor describes how his counseling provides the context for his preaching:

> I block out at least fifteen hours a week for counseling sessions, some of them on a one-to-one basis and others with groups. A colleague of mine, in discovering that commitment, remarked that it seemed to him an inefficient use of time. He felt that much more could be accomplished if that time were spent on sermon preparation or on speeches to be given to certain large groups; it would cost fewer minutes per person. From my point of view, however, those counseling appointments were an integral and indispensable element in my sermon preparation. They provide the material against which I am able to hear and appropriate and understand the Word, the context out of which my preaching has a chance to be relevant and alive and responsive to human need; and if I had not spent considerable time in such appointments, I'm not sure I would have "heard" from anyone as I sat down to write my sermon that

Thursday morning—or any other Thursday morning, for that
matter. The sermon is not an exposition of the Word alone but an
exposition of the Word in the context of the world.[6]

Time and again I have seen preachers fail to be heard in their
preaching because they failed to do the necessary pastoral care
that would have provided the proper context for congregational
hearing. William Sloane Coffin tells of the young social activist
preacher who got into trouble for his rather radical sermons. At a
heated vestry meeting, the young prophet's opponents finally
thought they had enough votes to call for his resignation. But
one man rose to speak in the pastor's behalf. "You all know that
I am, by nature, a conservative person," he said. "And I have
usually had political ideas that were diametrically opposed to
our pastor. But this young man stayed with me night and day
when my wife was ill. And when she died, only his patient care
and encouragement kept me going. During those hard times, I
learned his deep humanity and love. And so I'm going to try to
listen to him, to understand him, and to support him. For I will
always be indebted to him for what he did for me during my time
of need."

So pastoral care sometimes sets the context for effective
proclamation by helping reveal the humanity of the pastor who
is also prophet.

On the other hand, most preachers find that their counseling
experiences provide the best opportunity not only for helping
the parishioners know them but also for helping them know the
parishioners. Counseling vividly reveals the heights and depths
of the congregation's humanity to the preacher—and effective
preaching requires knowing people, not only in general but also
in quite specific detail. As we said earlier, such specific
knowledge requires listening to and observing one's parishioners
in their daily family life, work, frustrations, and dreams. As the
psychiatrist says in T. S. Eliot's play, *The Cocktail Party,*

I learn a good deal by merely observing you,
And letting you talk as long as you please,
And taking note of what you do not say.

When the people who hear the sermon know that *they* have
been truly heard by the pastor, and when the preacher can
convey in the sermon an accurate and honest feeling of "I know
what you are going through," then that preacher will in turn be
heard by the *people*.

The other day I visited a man who had been inactive in our
church for a number of years. Members of the congregation had
told me he was opposed to our denomination's stand on a
particular social issue.

At the beginning of my visit, he began talking very angrily
about our church becoming "downright communistic." He said
that first he withdrew his money, then he stopped attending to
protest the denomination's policies. He talked and talked,
criticizing everyone from the President to our bishop. He
accused me of "aiding and abetting those who want to destroy
our way of life."

I soon could feel my own anger rising. I began feeling
defensive. I was on the verge of doing some talking of my
own—telling him he was a racist, a bigot, and an extremist who
did not belong in the church. He could leave with my blessing.

Then I started to listen to his tirade with a bit more sensitivity.

"I don't know what's happening," he said. "I don't
understand it all. Do you know, I never had a weapon in this
house until a few years ago. Now I have two automatic rifles, a
shotgun, and a pistol. When *they* come up out of the city and try
to take my home away from me, I'll be ready. I'll be ready. I just
don't know where it's all going to end. No one seems to care
about me. I'm going to look out for myself since no one else is."

His words struck me: "No one seems to care. . . ." Suddenly
I saw him, not as a right-wing political extremist, not as the

racist, bigoted person his words showed him to be, but as a pitiful, frightened little boy crying out at a world he did not understand. From all that he could see, no one was in charge anymore, no one cared, no one was looking out for him—not even God.

I first wanted to "preach" to the symptoms of his sickness—the racism, bigotry, and extremism—to tell him that this was no way for a real Christian to feel. But sustained listening to him, as unpleasant as I found it, revealed the possible sickness beyond the symptoms. He was afraid. There in his hundred-thousand-dollar house and elegant living room with period furniture, he was little more than a terrified small boy, crouching in the corner out of fear of the dark.

Fear was more his problem than hate; hate arose out of fear. A sermon on racism, or Christian economics, or the virtue of social activism would be irrelevant to his plight. He needed hope. He needed faith that there is a God, that God cares, that God is still in control, that these strangers who are so feared are really brothers and sisters. In theological terms, I wondered if his inadequate eschatology had fostered his warped morality.

Leaving his house that day I wondered: How often have I approached human problems in a superficial way because I have not carefully diagnosed the human condition? How often have I preached something less than the Good News because I did not fully appreciate the depth of human need? How often have I not listened?

We preachers might be more intentional in sharing the insights of our listening within the sermon itself (using discretion, of course): "This week, in visiting in some of your homes, I discovered that many of you are feeling what I have been feeling lately—worry and confusion about the future. What does the future look like for you? Is there anything the Bible has to say to people like us who face such uncertain prospects?" or, "Here we are, starting another new year together. Some of you have already told me your New Year's resolutions. Many of you, I have learned, have decided to do some things differently in your lives. It's a time for fresh starts and new beginnings. In a way, a time like this is a gift of God—our God who is a God of change, fresh starts, beginnings. . . ."

Kierkegaard once warned preachers that the task of the religious speaker is "to present a human being as he is in daily life," not as an ideal type or some detached *homo religiosis*.

> The speaker who does not know how the task looks in daily life and in the living-room, might just as well keep still, for Sunday glimpses into eternity lead to nothing but wind . . . in the living-room the battle must be fought, for the victory consists precisely in the living-room becoming a sanctuary.[7]

When preaching degenerates into a nonempathetic exercise in which the preacher uses the sermon to prod, manipulate, cajole, or shame people into certain responses he or she deems appropriate, one wonders if we are listening to a preacher who is really a pastor. Such preaching devalues persons, acts as if the preacher is the Big Daddy (or Big Mama) figure who knows what is best for the wayward children, as if the preacher were not involved in the sins and shortcomings that are the subject of the sermon. Only when the preacher stands in solidarity with his or her people, identifies with them, and makes it clear that the Word addresses not only *you* but *us*—only then can the true character of the Word be heard. Such solidarity and identification are the fruits of patient and earnest pastoral contact with one's parishioners—contact which can be achieved, to a large extent, in our pastoral counseling activities.

HOW PREACHING AIDS COUNSELING

One of the major problems for pastoral counseling as it has developed in American churches in this century is its tendency to rely on secular therapeutic techniques and methods to the point where these therapies are sometimes substituted for Christian pastoral care. Sometimes while pastoral counselors were borrowing insights and methods from secular therapies, these therapies were substituted for the gospel. Fortunately, current writers and practitioners of pastoral counseling and pastoral psychology have become aware of this identity problem and are seeking to reclaim what is distinctively Christian, distinctively pastoral, about Christian pastoral counseling.[8]

Preaching can be a helpful symbolic means of identifying the context and identity of whatever counseling we do. The pastoral counselor derives his or her identity and authority from the exercise of the more public ministerial roles. Every time pastors lead their congregations in worship and preaching, they renew and symbolize, in a public and traditionally recognizable way, their official capacity as representative persons ordained to bear the wisdom, resources, tradition, and authority of the Christian faith. Such churchly resources as ritual, Scripture, tradition, community, forgiveness, and moral teaching can be valuable resources in helping persons who are undergoing stress, bereavement, guilt, and tragedy, as well as the day-to-day growing pains of life itself. The representational, symbolic character of our preaching and worship leadership can help deepen our counseling, pushing beyond the merely psychological or merely personal to deeper theological, communal, and ultimate questions.

When troubled persons come to a counselor who is also a preacher, many of them may do so from an unconscious desire to have their needs met within a more ultimate, moral, and theological context than may be possible in merely secular, exclusively psychologically-oriented counseling. Pastoral counselors would therefore be wise to explore the possible reasons that persons choose to receive the counsel of one who is also worship leader, ordained person, and preacher.

Of course, certain types of preaching and certain aspects inherent in all preaching can have a potentially negative influence upon our pastoral counseling and care of people. The authoritarian, judgmental, aloof stance of some preaching; the distance between the preacher and the parishioners that is encouraged by some preaching; or the irrelevant banality of some preaching can do more to frustrate our pastoral care of persons than it does to help.

Because most people will probably experience their pastor as a preacher before they have a chance to know their pastor as a counselor, we might do well to look upon our preaching as precounseling activity. What kind of precounseling setting do we construct in our preaching? Do we present ourselves as someone who always has easy answers to every problem, who never has problems of his or her own, who is more interested in telling people what they ought to do rather than in hearing who people really are?

The following episode happened to me after I had preached a sermon arising out of the words of the prophet Hosea, who condemned the worship of Baal. The sermon was entitled "Sex: Gift or God?" and attempted to portray a Christian attitude toward human sexuality.

Late one afternoon a young man in my congregation came to my office and said he would like to talk to me. When I asked what he wanted to talk about, he said he merely wanted to discuss his future plans for college. After about an hour of rather rambling conversation, I told him I wasn't sure he was really getting to whatever problem it was he wished to talk about. He blushed, and after some faltering comments, he said that he would like to respond to my sermon of the previous Sunday. He said he had never heard a preacher dare to preach about sex before and wondered what all the "little old ladies" had to say to me after the sermon. I told him I had not had any negative responses but I was curious what his reponse was. He said he liked the sermon. When I asked him what he liked about it, he blushed again and said he was simply surprised to hear a preacher talk so bluntly about sex. After about thirty minutes more of rambling conversation, he finally got around to the issue he wished to speak about. He informed me that he had been engaging in a homosexual relationship with an older man for the past few weeks. He claimed his relationship was not causing him any problems but he was curious as to what I thought about homosexuality. From here we launched into a rather lengthy discussion about his feelings on the matter, what the Bible had to say about the subject, and what might be best for his own life.

I gathered from this pastoral counseling episode that my sermon had provided the context for this young man's deciding that his pastor might be someone with whom he could talk over his ambivalent feelings about his own sexuality. Because the subject had been discussed in a sermon, he had evidently decided that I would be open to a deeper and more personal discussion of the subject in pastoral counseling. At any rate, this conversation struck me as an example of how preaching can sometimes open the door to, or create the context for, pastoral counseling. It would be interesting to know how many people seek out a pastor for counseling after the door has been opened for them within a sermon.

Even though much of our preaching does contribute to our opportunities for pastoral counseling, I find it necessary to keep the counseling function and the preaching function distinct in the practice of ministry. I do not mean to exchange Fosdick's characterization of preaching as "counseling on a group scale" for a characterization of preaching as "precounseling on a group scale."

Although counseling is an important pastoral task, preaching is a more central function. It is central because in preaching (as well as in the other public, traditional, and symbolic liturgical functions) the minister's identity as an ordained, official, community person is most clearly visible. For the pastoral counselor to be simply a well-intentioned helper of other people is not enough—not enough even for him or her to be a skillful helper of other people. The pastoral counselor is unique in that he or she works from within the context of the church: its values, traditions, beliefs, ethics, ritual, and common life. When our counseling ignores or devalues this unique context, it is less than Christian pastoral counseling. Preaching aids pastoral counseling by making that context visible and explicit.

In my own pastoral counseling I have experienced difficulty in relating the values, traditions, beliefs, ethics, ritual, and common life of the church to the needs of specific individuals who come for counseling. Perhaps my difficulty is due to the way I was trained to counsel. I was schooled in the Rogerian, nondirective approach. I was urged to listen, to let the "client" do the talking, to not intrude upon the client with my value judgments and advice, to avoid preaching to the troubled person.

This nondirective approach was helpful for many of us. It helped us listen, respect the integrity and inner resources of persons, and avoid offering pat answers and insensitive solutions to difficult problems.

But this nondirective approach was also harmful when it led us pastors to avoid giving *any* direction, guidance, or judgment within the context of counseling. As Don Browning observed, many problem-laden people seek out a pastor for counseling because they sense that a major source of contemporary psychological problems is that many persons lack adequate values, goals, direction, and judgments. Is it not reasonable for problem-laden people who are within the faith-community to assume that their pastor might be a valuable resource for discerning Christian values, goals, direction, and judgments for their lives?

So preaching aids pastoral counseling by constantly reminding both pastor and congregation of the ecclesial, theological, and moral context of our pastoral care.

A friend of mine struggled with the relationship between counseling and preaching in his own ministry within the context of the problem of divorce:

> I looked at the lessons for next Sunday as I started to think about preparing a sermon. The Gospel: Mark 10:2-12. I shuddered. "You will not catch me preaching on divorce," I said to myself—too many divorces of our own right here in this congregation. I wouldn't touch that text with a ten-foot pole. But I thought again. Why not? After all, Jesus' words on divorce *are* in the Bible and they are part of the lesson for this Sunday. And divorce *is* a major problem in this congregation. I also know, from my own counseling experiences, that most of my people who were contemplating a divorce or who had been divorced had Jesus' words about the subject preying on their minds. What was there about the divorce problem that made me deal with it in a pastoral counseling session but not in a sermon? On the other hand, what was there about my pastoral counseling sessions with divorced people that made me avoid any mention of the biblical testimony on divorce?
>
> After much prayer and consideration, I decided to level with the people, to admit to them that I was tempted to ignore this Sunday's text on divorce rather than preach on it. I would tell them why I thought I wanted to avoid the text: it sounds so harsh and judgmental when I read it in the context of all the good and sincere Christians I know right here in my own church who are going through the pain of divorce. Then I would, in the sermon, try to speak about the context of Jesus' words on divorce, what I think they meant then and what I think they mean for us now.
>
> I decided that I had to preach from that text, or I wasn't being true to my calling as a preacher. I decided that I had to preach from that text, or I wasn't being true to my calling as a counselor. Here was a pressing, contemporary, difficult human need that the Bible was addressing and with which my church was struggling—and what better place to begin to confront that need than in the sermon?

Do you remember my writing earlier that I wondered how many troubled people seek out a pastor for counseling after the door has been opened for them in a sermon? In closing, I wonder how many of us preachers are led to a bold confrontation with the truth, the comfort, and the hard demands of the gospel after the door has been opened for *us* within a counseling session?

III. THE PREACHER AS COMMUNITY PERSON

When an ordained minister steps into the pulpit, what is the difference between his or her speaking and that of any other baptized Christian? What is there about ordination that somehow makes this Christian's preaching special?

Some say that the ordained person is specially called by God to preach. But *all* Christians are called to proclaim the gospel, to evangelize, to spread the Good News in word and deed. All Christians share the call to the "royal priesthood" by virtue of their baptism (1 Peter 2:9). All Christians are free to interpret the Bible, to be led by the Spirit, to witness to the truth of the gospel as it is revealed to them. So what makes the pulpit witnessing of this ordained Christian different from the public witness of any other Christian?

The Roman Catholic church once said that priests had been given a special *character indelebilis*: an indelible, holy imprint in the ordination rite. More recently some writers on the ordained ministry have claimed that pastors, although not necessarily holier than the mass of ordinary Christians, do have unique areas of competence and skill—"functional responsibility," as Seward Hiltner called it. [1] James Glasse contended that ordained persons were skilled "professionals" who had certain unique skills that they purveyed to the laity.[2] Urban Holmes called the minister the "sacramental person" who embodies "the expectancy of the transcendent with the immanence of the personal."[3] David Switzer even called the minister the "clown" who presents "him/herself as a *person*, as a person of *faith*, an expression of which is also his/her vocation, and by being aware of and utilizing the responses of the other persons to him/her as a symbol."[4]

In my opinion, all such talk of alleged specialness among the ordained clergy deflects our attention from the central function and historic basis of the ordained ministry:

> The ordained ministry is a function of the Christian community. An ordained minister is an official of the community, a representative, a designated leader. With my Protestant heritage, I recognize that an ordained minister should be, must be, called by God. . . . But with Calvin, I recognize a "twofold call" to the presbyterate. God calls us, and the church calls us . . . the call of the community . . . is the currently neglected aspect of our ministerial identity. An ordained minister is an official of the community . . . the central matter is in the office, in the officialness of the ordained minister's activities. To put it bluntly, there is no difference when a priest baptizes, preaches, forgives, blesses, prays, counsels, or supports compared to when any other Christian does these things—save in the officialness of the action.[5]

The Christian community is therefore the source of the ordained ministry. Without that community and its mission, the ordained pastoral ministry would not be needed.

What does the New Testament say about this matter? It shows no interest in our later debates over the validity of orders. It depicts ministers not so much as *in* orders as *under* orders. It speaks of what orders are for—their function, the ends to which this office is directed:

> Officials are neither desirable nor necessary for any community except for the realization of the community's purposes, the pursuit

of communal goals. All groups designate leaders, . . . not to make leaders but to make a group. Leadership is not an optional matter for a group, particularly a group that wishes to perform any significant task. Jesus knew this. Jesus not only preached, healed, judged, and released; he formed community. He empowered a group to turn the world upside down. He commissioned and sent forth in order to enlarge that new community.[6]

From the earliest days of the church, presbyters and overseers (priests, elders, bishops, pastors) were designated to concentrate upon the community-forming as well as the community-criticizing dimensions of the faith. As Paul notes, edification—upbuilding—is the central task of the designated officials of the church:

The pastor is the one who is charged with seeing—in all aspects of pastoral care—individual lives within the context of the whole; to bear the sometimes heavy burden of the community's tradition; to note the presence of inequality, division, and diversity; to create the conditions necessary for consensus; to foster a climate where reconciliation can occur; to judge the potentially demonic aspects of our "togetherness"; to ask whether the community we seek and attain is a specifically *Christian* community; to distinguish between his or her personal preferences and what community cohesion, maintenance, and critique require.[7]

Therefore, to understand the specialness of the ordained minister's preaching, we must refer to the officialness of the ordained minister. When an ordained person preaches, the difference between his or her preaching and that of other baptized Christians is not that the ordained person is holier, or more skillful, or more led by the spirit, or more intelligent; the difference is in the officialness. The ordained person is communally, officially, publicly, and symbolically designated the "community person."

GETTING IT TOGETHER AND KEEPING IT
TOGETHER THROUGH THE PULPIT

From its beginning, the Christian church has been deeply concerned with unity and union, community and communion. Perhaps in praying that "they all might be one," Christ knew that a vision so bold as his, a task so great as the one to which he called his disciples, a message so powerful as the one he preached, could not be sustained without a body of believers who spoke and acted as one. "There is one body and one spirit, just as you were called to the one hope that belongs to your call, one Lord, one faith, one baptism, one God and Father of us all" (Ephesians 4:4-6a).

Within the congregation, the community-forming functions of the pastor are many. But in this chapter I want to focus on one of those communal functions that relate to preaching—congregational unity—in the hope of suggesting other ways the preacher functions as "community person." For a local congregation to be a functioning, fulfilling, faithful church, it must be a unified congregation, and for congregational unity there are six requisites, all of which relate to preaching.[8] Using the experiences of some of my fellow preachers I hope to illustrate how congregational unity can be fostered in the integrative preaching of the community person.

1. *Common Sense of Identity.* The congregation must know who it is and to whom it belongs. It must be able to define itself and its boundaries. In recent years many liberal mainline denominations have played down denominational distinctiveness in favor of more generalized, universally acceptable, ecumenical values. Many of these same groups are now experiencing a crisis of identity. They have forgotten who they are.

Also, as American churches play down some of their former theological tenets and biblical ideas, they often seek identity elsewhere. "First Baptist is a friendly church," they may say. Or, "First Methodist is concerned about our community." But none of these claims designates a distinctively *Christian* church. Identity—uniquely Christian identity—must be tested against historical, biblical, ecclesial, and theological standards of judgment. Listen to one of my fellow pastors:

> Every couple of years I set aside about a four to five week period to preach a series of sermons which I call, "This We Believe." I tell the congregation that this is a time for us to reflect together on the basics of the Christian faith, the basic beliefs of Christians. During this period, all adult and older youth church school groups are urged to use a denominational study book on our beliefs. In my sermons, I try to express, in as simple and concrete a way as possible, the distinctive, basic beliefs we share as Christians.

Through preaching, we come to know who we are. We define our particular story, our name, the truth claims unique to our way of looking at things. What one psychologist said of worship in general can be applied to preaching in particular:

> Worship is increasingly understood in terms of a rehearsal of the sense of one's identity as a member of a particular community of believers. The content of the liturgy expresses the beliefs and values of a particular community, and the experience of the liturgy in common reminds a person about where he belongs and finds his identity.[10]

2. Common Authority. In times of internal conflict, the congregation must have some creed, text, person, or constitution to which it can appeal—something by which belief and behavior are judged, some final arbiter. This is the final goal or purpose that guides a congregation and makes its gatherings specifically Christian.

A congregation that suffers from a lack of common authority finds its life detrimentally affected in a number of ways. For instance, without a commonly recognized authority to which everyone refers and defers, arguments are resolved only with difficulty. In such a situation, debate is often carefully avoided out of fear that it will be divisive rather than productive. The congregation attempts to keep everything polite, genteel, and cheerful, lest the group disintegrate during arguments because there is no authority to which differing points of view can appeal.

Congregations that lose the Bible or some other historic, basic affirmation of faith are forced to seek their common authority elsewhere. Authority therefore often comes to reside in the pastor or a lay leader of the congregation. In the absence of theologically based authority, standards that are secular, generalized, or culturally defined may become normal for the congregation: "It really doesn't matter what we believe as long as we are sincere." This is what one of my fellow pastors believes:

> I think it is important to let a congregation know that you are preaching from the Bible. I believe people are hungry for the Bible, and like to see their preacher wrestling with the Bible. I let the lectionary guide me in my preaching, publishing the texts for my sermons a month in advance in the church newsletter and urging people to read and study these texts at home. In all this I want to convey to my people that I am servant of the Word, that my preaching is to be judged by its faithfulness to Scripture. Sometimes I let people know how hard it is for me to understand and to preach from the tough texts of the Bible. I let them know it in the sermon itself, sometimes. This reminds them, "It's our book and we stand under it—whether we always like what it says or not!"

3. *Common Memory.* The unified congregation has a shared story, a common history, through which it understands itself and its mission. Every unified group has a carefully nurtured, frequently recalled history, a pantheon of heroes, sacred places, and events. This common history gives a congregation its roots, its authority, its identity.

But we live in a uniquely ahistorical culture that tends to value youth and newness over age and established work. Concern for the past is often judged to be mere antiquarianism or backward-looking conservatism. We are a mobile society that is always making room for newcomers rather than valuing older persons. This attitude has given us a rootless, disjointed, alienated feeling. Without a past, we know not who we are in the present and feel under a strain about the future. We suffer from corporate amnesia and its debilitating affects. One of my pastor friends expresses this feeling this way:

> Although I don't think a preacher ought to push this too far, I believe in an unashamedly "historical" sermon from time to time—such as on Reformation Sunday, All Saints Day, or the church Founder's Day. This lets us celebrate the saints who have gone before us. I also take delight in using illustrations from the lives and events of the past in my sermons. I try particularly to use "local" saints right in our own town—people whose lives point the way for faithfulness in our own time.

4. Common Vision. As a common memory identifies where a group has been, so a common vision identifies where the congregation should be or hopes to be in the future. It must dream, envision, plan, boldly step out into the future, look beyond immediate needs, fears, and contingencies.

Christianity has long been an eschatological, end-of-time faith. The New Testament was written in a time-frame that saw Christians living in a new age in which God's future was unfolding with power and wonder. For the church to be content to oil today's ecclesiastical machinery is not enough. It must strain forward into God's future, seeing things as they can be and as God is making them, rather than exclusively seeing things as they are now.

> Many of my people are afraid of what lies ahead, especially the young adults. I've recently been impressed, particularly in my

premarital counseling sessions, with how many young adults fear a future of shortages, threats of nuclear war, rising unemployment. This is the generation that knew affluence and rising expectations. Now they are realizing that in the future we must cut back. In times like these, I've rediscovered the power of much of the biblical apocalypticism and end-of-time images. I never thought I would see much value, say, in the Book of Revelation. But I think in a time when people are fearful or hopeless, it's a great time to talk about what a Christian's hopes really are. What is the Christian hope when the world is, so to speak, "going to hell in a handbasket?"

5. *Common Shared Life Together*. A congregation must share the intimacy, mutual feeling, and fellowship that is the sign of the presence of God's kingdom in our midst. We live in a nation caught between its strong individualism and its deep yearning for community. Many people seek and join a church because they yearn to be part of a group that cares. From its beginning, the proof that the church was of divine origin and substance was that outsiders exclaimed, "See how they love one another!"

Since the activist nineteen-sixties, many congregations have stressed congregational involvement in the needs of the surrounding community and have played down the importance of common, shared life together. Their energies have gone into what they called community outreach. But the church must not neglect its own internal needs. It must take care to *create* a community as well as to *serve* the wider community.

The preacher can do many things to build a sense of congregational unity and care. Mentioning those who are sick, or suffering bereavement or some other troubled time, is a natural thing to do in the pastoral prayer. This helps remind people that other Christians' needs are my needs too. Beyond this, I think we need to be more intentional as preachers in celebrating congregational victories. Most churches I have been associated with are so impressed by all that they fail to do, all the ways they fail to be the church, that they never acknowledge the good things they are doing. We preachers are often guilty of harping on the negative. I think a sermon is a good time to step back and say, "Let's thank God that this happened here. Let's celebrate a victory together." The end of a successful financial campaign, the Sunday before high school graduation, when someone joins the church, when the congregation takes a stand on some difficult issue, even many of our funerals—these are approriate times for congregational victory sermons.

6. *Common Shared Life in the World.* A Christian congregation is called to be more than a cozy mutual admiration society, an isolated enclave of like-minded friends. It is also called to be a visible witness to the ever-coming kingdom of God in the world.

The church lives in the tension of having to love and win the world, yet not be of the world. In recent years, many have come to believe that a concern for congregational identity, unity, and community is antithetical to concern with serving the world. But a congregation, like individuals, must love itself before it is capable of loving others. A congregation cannot love its neighbors in a vibrant, committed way until it has first learned to love its own witness, tradition, message, and life together. It must be confident and optimistic about itself before it will be motivated to share itself with the world. Unless a congregation experiences the gospel within its own congregational life, it very likely will have little gospel to share with anyone else.

Congregational involvement in ministry to the world can be a source of congregational unity and vitality. Even when involvement and activism bring conflict, the congregation's response to that conflict may create a more unified body. The conflict may provide the occasion for working through congregational identity and faith. It may result in deeper commitment, risk, and involvement when the congregation experiences itself not only as a unified, friendly, caring group but also as a visible witness to the kingdom of God in the world.

I remember the time we took on the local police department. It all began with our ministry to the local jail. When we got inside, we found things we didn't like: police using excessive force, harassment of younger prisoners, terrible living conditions. When we tried to say something to the chief about it, he in effect told us to stick to running a church and he would run the jail. That really got some of our people stirred up. We gave interviews to the local newspaper, wrote the state law enforcement division, and in general made things hot for the chief. He finally backed down and said he would ask for more money and outside help for the jail. I think I used two or three sermons during that crisis to let the congregation know why some of us thought that, as Christians, we ought to be involved in this fight. I also used one sermon as a sort of celebration of the victory after we won—patting the members on the back, if you will. Not everyone was in favor of what we did. There was much discussion pro and con within the congregation itself. That's a great opportunity to let the crisis inform the sermon.

As the official community person, the preacher has many different community concerns other than congregational unity alone: integrating new members into the congregation, speaking on behalf of the congregation on certain occasions, refereeing in times of congregational conflict, guiding the congregation through times of courage. I hope that these observations on congregational unity and these preachers' reports on their own experiences of integrating community concerns with preaching suggest some ways in which preaching can be a communal and unifying activity.

BUILDING UP THE BODY

Throughout these thoughts on the centrality of preaching, I have tried to stress that preaching is not an individualistic enterprise. The preacher is not a star actor trying to entice, cajole, or for that matter, scold, berate, or manipulate an audience "out there." A preacher stands "up there" because the congregation and God working through the congregation have elected to put the preacher there. They have elected to put the preacher there not simply because he or she has something interesting to say, or is attractive, or has an enticing personality, or is a courageous prophet. The preacher is there for all of us, a community person whose preaching is an extension, a function of the community of faith. All other claims for the authority of preaching are egocentric, idiosyncratic, and less than the power and breadth of Christian edification.

Sometimes we preachers get confused about our proper task. We think the congregation wants from us a baring of our own soul, a private testimony of our own spiritual ups and downs, a true confession of "A Day in the Life of Pastor X." Such personal, self-centered preaching may do the preacher some good, but it is largely irrelevant to the most fundamental needs of the congregation. Recent encouragement for preachers to simply "share yourself in the sermon" is compatible with the narcissistic tendencies of our age but is, as I have attempted to show in this chapter, opposed to the historic basis for the ordained ministry or contemporary Christian need.

I therefore part company with David Switzer when he says that the main "symbol" pastors have to give their parishioners is themselves.[11] Thank God, we preachers have something to preach other than ourselves! Any pastors who have only themselves to preach in sermons, to offer in pastoral care situations, to gather the community around, are sure to run dry—no matter how great their personality or how empathetic their care.

We preach Christ, not ourselves (2 Cor. 4:4). We are "stewards of the mysteries of God," not merely sharers of our well-meaning good deeds. Therein lies our true authority as preachers or pastors, our true vocation.

When preaching is not central, the congregation invariably drifts from momentary fad to fad, or gathers itself around some enticing personality, or contents itself with being a sort of religious club. We do not discover the identity of the church by rooting around within our own psyches or by buying into whatever the culture happens to be peddling at the moment. We must tell the identity of the church to the church, in each generation, for the church does not know her own name unless she is told that name. We must tell the story and distinguish it from a myriad of other stories. This is how preaching is the lifeblood and rallying point, the continual recalling and re-presentation of who we are and what we are to be doing.

As Barth said of preaching within the congregation:

> To build up the Church means to rebuild each time from foundation to roof. The Church has to be remaking itself continually; continually the orders given have to be accepted, obedience has constantly to be learned again. "By obedience to obedience" is the journey of the Christian. The Church is a community placed under Revelation and built up by hearing the Word of God, built up by the grace of God in order that it may live.[12]

The goal of the community person as preacher is not only to edify the community's identity, unity, and life together but also to enable the community to move out beyond itself to others. As P. T. Forsyth said a generation ago, the greatest preacher is not the individual preacher but the church itself. The goal of the preacher is not only to preach the gospel to the church but to enable the church to preach the gospel to the world.

> The one great preacher in history . . . is the church. And the first business of the individual preacher is to enable the Church to preach. . . . He is to preach to the Church from the Gospel so that with the Church he may preach the Gospel to the world. He is so to preach to the Church that he shall also preach through the Church. That is to say, he must be a sacrament to the Church, that with the Church he may become a missionary to the world.[13]

To call pastors the community person is to remind us that our preaching is a ministry of the church. Our unique service to that church is to articulate the faith of the community, the faith we hold and that holds us. At times we preach to convert, to win the outsiders in the world who, with those in the church, are also objects of Christ's salvation and love. We preach for decision, first commitment, and evangelization. But let us remember that we also preach to confirm and to celebrate the work of Christ among his own. We don't have to make the church—Christ has already done that. Our task, in the word of Richard Neuhaus, is "to help the Church recognize and actualize what God has already declared it to be."[14]

IV. THE PREACHER AS TEACHER

In his influential book *Why Conservative Churches Are Growing*, Dean Kelley says that one of the reasons for the recent remarkable growth of conservative churches in American Protestantism is that they take seriously the need of people to find meaning in and make sense out of life.[1] They take seriously the teaching task of the church. They help their members put things together, make sense out of the world. Although we do not often think of the so-called conservative churches as being primarily interested in education and teaching, and they probably do not often think of themselves as teachers and educators, their growth reminds us that one of humanity's basic needs is the need for meaning. Whenever the church addresses questions of meaning and helps us put things together into a configuration that makes sense and helps us order our lives, the church is teaching. Whenever the preacher helps people make sense out of the world and their lives, the preacher is also teaching.

PREACHING AND TEACHING

In his book on preaching in the early church, C. H. Dodd distinguished between preaching *(kerygma)* and teaching *(didache)*. Teaching was said to be addressed to persons already established in the faith. Preaching was addressed mainly to non-Christians. Preaching was proclamation. Teaching was doctrinal instruction or moral exhortation.[2]

Recent writers have challenged Dodd's sharp distinction between preaching and teaching in the early church—or in the church today. Although Dodd's distinction does help characterize the respective functions of early instruction and early proclamation, it too narrowly conceives of the function of either preaching or teaching in the church. Nothing in the New Testament indicates that early Christian teachers and preachers had different messages. They all were delivering the gospel. They all had goals that could be commonly described as evangelistic. They all had as their common purpose the upbuilding of the community.

When does genuine Christian preaching stop being proclamation and start being teaching? How is it possible to proclaim the gospel without doing teaching, enlightenment and clarification, construction of meaning? Who can say when learning begins or ends in any sermon? Preaching becomes *Christian* preaching whenever it is concerned with the *kerygma*. The truth of the gospel makes Christian preaching.

Christian preaching is also Christian teaching whenever it helps people understand, internalize, and apply God's Word to their lives. When preaching becomes teaching, it helps us understand the implications of the Christian tradition, canon, and doctrine for our lives; it helps us evaluate our lives in the light of that tradition in order to be better equipped for faithful life in the church and the world.[3]

Sometimes doctrinal preaching may be for the benefit of those outside the church: as apologetics, witnessing to the superiority of Christian faith truth claims over other contenders for humanity's allegiance. At other times it may be for the upbuilding of the church: helping Christians grow and mature in their faith. But both types of preaching are preaching that is also teaching.

Many pastors are afraid of intentionally doctrinal preaching. They suspect that lay persons are less than interested in hearing theological treatises on Sunday morning—and they are probably right! It sounds so deadly dull. The very term *doctrinal preaching* sounds like a homiletical license to pontificate to the laity on fine points of doctrine, to overwhelm the unenlightened with the pastor's erudition. Thus doctrinal preaching can be a questionable enterprise indeed. Why not save such educative work for the church school classroom and keep the pulpit free for pure proclamation?

And so Colin Morris warns preachers about being tempted, on Trinity Sunday, to launch into the murky waters of theological exposition:

> Trinity Sunday is the preacher's Waterloo. If he is prudent he will go down with a strategic bout of influenza the preceding day. If he suffers from a stern sense of duty, he will be forced to tie himself in verbal knots grappling with the ultimate mystery of God's Nature. Indeed, the Church could make an honest penny charging militant atheists an admission fee for the pleasure of seeing and hearing Christian preachers battle their way through an intellectual maze, which, at whatever point they enter it, soon has them hopelessly lost.[4]

The pitfalls of doctrinal preaching are primarily these: (1) that we tend to compartmentalize doctrinal preaching into a set type of preaching that merely intellectualizes, rationalizes, and dogmatizes the faith, thus reducing the gospel to a set of merely intellectual propositions; (2) that the preacher will become so enamored with various fine points of doctrine that he or she neglects the basic *kerygma*, the evangel. The gospel event becomes an abstraction. The result is a lecture that may be interesting, even mildly important, but not of ultimate, life-changing importance. Such preaching may elicit a nod of assent or intellectual approval from people, but it does not engage the will and call forth response. This is less than the fullness of Christian preaching. Preaching is not merely the public pronouncement of theology. "Theology constitutes a science, proclamation constitutes the church," is how Gerhard Ebeling distinguishes the two activities.[5]

But even with these pitfalls in mind, the pastor should also keep in mind that she or he is the chief interpreter, the main Christian educator, the resident theologian in the congregation. Most congregations will be flattered when their pastor asks them to stretch their minds, to expand their images and concepts of the faith, to grow in their knowledge and understanding. They are also pleased when they think their pastor dares to grapple with the issues and ideas that trouble them. Such pastoral tackling of the tough questions and great concepts of faith is not mere intellectual calisthenics; it is pastoral care of the highest order. "Don't talk down to us," one of my members told me. "Life is too complicated for preachers to make it sound simple."

Pastors preach frankly doctrinal or teaching sermons because they are convinced that it is wrong to say, "It doesn't matter what you believe as long as you're sincere," that their people will be helped by having their concepts refined, by growing beyond immature or inadequate ideas and images, by receiving some images and ideas through which to confront the mysteries of life. We engage in doctrinal preaching because what a person believes does make a difference—sincerity has little to do with it. All sorts of sincere folk hold wrong ideas, and their lives are stunted or hurt thereby.

I remember the young widow whose husband was struck down most unexpectedly in the prime of his life, leaving her with two young children. When I heard of his death, I rushed to her side. I was a bit surprised that her first words to me were,

"Tell me again all you said in that sermon a few weeks ago about God's will and sickness."

I was surprised because she was not an intellectual woman, in the strictest sense of the word, and I expected her to be in the emotional throes of grief. She was, I was soon to find, but at this point her grief was as much intellectual as emotional. "How could God do a thing like this to us?" was the question I heard behind her questions. Was this God's will? What kind of God could do this? What does God want us to do now?

In recent years I have noted that some pastoral psychologists and clinical pastoral education supervisors around the seminary have often urged students to lay aside their intellectual abilities and merely empathize, share their feelings with and simply be with troubled persons. Every pastor knows the limitation of words and ideas in times of personal crisis and the value of empathetic presence. And sometimes a warm heart and a kindly pastoral hand upon a troubled person's shoulder are enough.

But at other times words are crucially important. A time of acute crisis of grief is usually not the time to expound on the Christian view of life and afterlife. But it is a safe bet that at some time in the grieving process bereaved persons will be asking questions such as, Why did this happen to me? Will I ever see my father again? What is the meaning in all of this? Those are intellectual questions that relate to specific doctrines and ideas within the Christian faith. Therefore at some time, perhaps in the funeral sermon or even in a Sunday sermon, the caring pastor might like to speak to those questions and bring the resources of the Christian tradition to bear on these people's needs. When the preacher does so, preaching will become teaching.

To return to Colin Morris's advice on the dangers of preaching on the doctrine of the Trinity, an illustration from my own experience, although not refuting the pitfalls of doctrinal preaching, at least raises questions about Morris's claim that

Trinity Sunday is "the preacher's Waterloo." A few years ago I
had to face the question of what to preach on that Sunday. After
much thought I decided to give the old doctrine a try. This is
how my sermon began:

> The doctrine of the Trinity—the doctrine that says we experience
> God as Father, Son, and Holy Spirit. Who thinks much about it
> these days? Who understands it? Who cares? How many sermons
> have you heard on the Trinity? Not many, I suspect.
>
> And I bet that right now you're saying to yourself, No sermons on
> the doctrine of the Trinity are enough for me!
>
> So you don't ever think about the Trinity. But I'll bet you often
> think about God. Everybody thinks about God, I suppose. Even
> those who say they don't believe in God—I suspect they wonder
> sometimes, Is there a God? What is God like?
>
> The doctrine of the Trinity is simply the church talking about
> what it believes God is like. Today is a good day to do some thinking
> about how we experience God.

I moved from this beginning to speak about the ways we all
experience God in our daily lives: as a nurturing, caring parent;
as a mysterious and ever-present power; as the historical man,
Jesus of Nazareth. I then cited a few examples of contemporary
limited notions about God that the Trinity seeks to enlarge and
correct: the then-contemporary Jesus movement, which
emphasized Jesus as a warm, personal friend without
remembering God the Creator, Redeemer, and Father of all;
the neo-charismatic movement, which sometimes forgot the
ethical, earthly demands of Jesus the Son in its infatuation with
the ethereal, spectacular workings of the Spirit; the established,
mainline church, which often settles down to a God who is
merely a benevolent, indulgent parent but never an ethically
demanding Lord or prodding Spirit. My point was that, even
though it is often difficult to balance the various modes of God's
work in our own lives, the Trinity reminds us that our daily
experiences of God transcend our definitions and images of
God, that even our most all-encompassing definitions must be

broadened and judged by the church's historic definitions of God such as we have in the doctrine of the Trinity:

> God the Father, God the Son, God the Holy Spirit. Your mind and my mind may not be big enough to do justice to all that at once, but we must try. It is the same God, working in us and through us and in spite of us.

I believe that unashamedly doctrinal preaching works best when the preacher indicates that the teaching is being done within the sermon as a concrete response to a perceived need within the congregation for deeper understanding of some issue:

> I'm sure you read recently about the group of Christians in a nearby city who refused to pay their taxes as a protest against the defense policies of our government. Such civil disobedience in the name of Christianity raises questions. What does our church believe about such acts of protest?
>
> Or,
>
> Today we baptize Jane and Tom, thus receiving them into God's family, the church. Each new baptism is a good time to remember our own baptism, to think about the meaning of that event and further penetrate its meaning for our lives. Today I will use these words from Paul to . . .

Teaching is not always an intellectual activity. In recent years, educators have gained a new appreciation for the intuitive, affective modes of consciousness. The Christian life is probably much more an act of the heart and the will than it is a set of propositions to be mastered in the mind. A poem, a picture, or a play can teach as well as a closely reasoned discourse. To return to our opening definition of teaching, *Christian preaching is also Christian teaching whenever it helps people understand, internalize, and apply God's Word to their lives.* That understanding, internalization, and application is never a merely cerebral affair, particularly when we are teaching the gospel. We must not aid our people in intellectualizing the faith, in turning it into a set of noble but abstract propositions and concepts that we are free to discuss politely and then walk away from. The truth of Christianity that John's Gospel says will make us free is, not a concept, but a *person*. The truth of the gospel is personal: a confrontation with a Man, not merely the explication of a message.

And so confrontation, clarification, and proclamation of this person, Jesus of Nazareth—crucified, buried, risen, and reigning—are the subject matter of Christian preaching and teaching. Our goal is a relationship, a way of life together, a pattern of obedience, not merely the assimilation of new and intriguing information. The preacher, whenever she or he teaches, is not an expert on things religious informing a group of learners. Instead, the preacher is a person who is sharing some of life's most intimate and mysterious experiences with other persons. Whenever that happens in a sermon and people better understand, internalize, and apply what they hear, Christian teaching has occurred.

The great prophet Washington Gladden called preachers of his day to be teachers, speakers of the truth. His words, spoken almost one hundred years ago, remind us of our teaching vocation as preachers:

> Christ said that the one supreme purpose of his mission to the world was that he might bear witness to the truth; and the same must always be the high calling of the servant of Christ. . . . Men are saved from being conformed to this world only when they are transformed by the renewing of their minds; and it is the minister's chief business to keep their minds well supplied with the truth by which this transformation is wrought.[6]

V. THE PREACHER AS PROPHET

Throughout this book I have stressed the value of intentionally *pastoral* preaching. I have contended that there are important reasons for integrating pastoral experiences, insights, and concerns with our preaching. Looking back over the foregoing chapters, I can see how one might get the impression that the best preachers are those well-meaning souls who go from house to house loving, caring, listening, observing, and in general doing good things for parishioners and keeping the ecclesiastical machinery oiled.

But if preachers are servants of the word—a word that not only soothes, assuages, encourages, and blesses but also judges, convicts, and demands—might not faithful service to that word at some time entail switching from the pastoral mode to the prophetic? Indeed, faithfulness to the word—to say nothing of faithfulness to the needs and expectations of most congregations—means that preachers must think of themselves not only as pastors but also as prophets. The centrality of the pulpit reminds pastors that their role is not merely to do nice things for nice people in the congregation; they are also to speak the truth in love, even when the truth hurts.

In recent years we have seen much stress on the preacher's

prophetic role. In my seminary days most of us took the term *pastor*, when applied to a minister, to designate a prophet who had become soft! We all wanted to be prophets: courageous speakers of the truth and social activists rather than tame, domesticated, keepers of congregations. Although some of this social activism seems to have cooled, the church and its ministry are fortunate that prophetic preaching and social witness, particularly that nurtured through liberation theology, continue to be major concerns.[1]

IDENTITY-INVOLVEMENT

The problem with some of our current social involvement is that many churches are in the throes of what theologian Jürgen Moltmann has characterized the "Identity-Involvement Dilemma." Moltmann notes that when the church becomes preoccupied with its identity and spends most of its energies looking at and restating who it is, it becomes a religious club, a self-satisfied enclave removed from the struggles of the world. On the other hand, when the church involves itself in social and political struggle, it tends to get swallowed up by secular movements and to lose its identity. It forgets why it is involved in the struggle, why it is involved as a *Christian* gathering. When the church allows, in that favorite phrase of the 1960s, "the world to set the agenda," it often forgets that God has called the meeting! The end result of this loss of identity in favor of involvement is what Moltmann calls "chameleon theology": adapting the church's faith to blend with its secular surroundings.[2]

One of the contentions of this book has been that as Christians come to know who they are, they naturally know what they ought to be doing. Identity, therefore, is the crucially important starting point for meaningful Christian involvement in the world. As I argued in chapter 3, we must foster a clearly identifiable and unified community of faith before we move out to serve the larger community that surrounds it.

But I have also seen, from firsthand experience and observation, that there is a sense in which our identity comes to us as the result of experiential learning, through what educators call action-reflection learning. Sometimes we find out who we are by becoming involved and experiencing ourselves as Christians trying to act and serve like Christians. There is a certain sense in which our identity as Christians comes not only by speaking and hearing the truth but also by doing the truth.

For many years American evangelical Protestantism said such things as, "We don't believe the church should work to save society. It should work to save individual souls. When these individual souls are saved, they will go back into society as individual Christians to convert the society." In recent social struggles many of us learned this was an unrealistic philosophy: thousands of sincere individual Christians see no relationship between their individual salvation and the needs of the world—particularly when they are part of a church that contents itself with applying the gospel only to the safe confines of individual lives, individual sins, individual needs, and individual salvation.

Is it possible for the church to really discover who it is, as the church, when it defines its identity apart from its mission and witness, its service and ministry? I doubt it. Because we sometimes discover who we are as Christians only when we are trying to live and act like Christians, the "Identity-Involvement Dilemma" can be a positive occasion for a mutual interplay of two central Christian claims that enrich and inform one another.

When the church engages in some pressing community problem and things do not change in spite of the church's best and most prayerful efforts, when Christians are forced to work alongside non-Christians in order to meet some social need, when the church's activism brings it face to face with the political and economic "powers and principalities of darkness" in this world, then the church is driven back to itself to ask, What does our faith say about this? Like Moses we ask, *Who are we* that we should be sent by God to call for liberation of the captives?

The asking of such questions is a prime opportunity for the preacher to proclaim the gospel. In this way congregational social concern and activist involvement help set the context for faithful preaching. This chapter will suggest some of the integrative possibilities that occur when the preacher is also prophet.

MORALIZING IN THE PULPIT

Although our preaching must be prophetic if it is to be faithful, much that passes for prophetic preaching is not without its pitfalls: the greatest danger is the age-old homiletical sin of moralizing. Elsewhere I have defined moralizing as occurring when,

> Preachers pick through the biblical tradition in hope of finding texts from which to draw simple moral inferences, usually ideals that the listeners should do or be. The gospel is presented in the form of suggestions for better living, principles for correct opinion, or obligations to be met. In moralizing, the gospel is usually distorted by the pastor's earnest attempt to find something relevant to say—some easy, straightforward plan of action to urge upon the people. Moralizing perverts Christian proclamation, because the gospel usually has to do with *God's* actions and plans, rather than ours.[3]

Obviously, moral concerns are found in the Bible and are the proper subject of preaching. Obviously, congregations need to be confronted with the moral and ethical demands of the gospel.

But, as Leander Keck says, "What is decisive, however, is whether this is done in a way that accords with the Bible's own way of understanding moral obligation."[4]

The Bible is not an assortment of moral precepts and examples. Most of the Bible is theocentric, that is, *God* is the center of the Bible's concern—God's dealings with humanity, not simply humanity's dealings with humanity. The Bible's concerns are usually more fundamental, more theological, more overarching, than moralistic preaching makes them out to be.

So the sermon is not merely an exercise in telling people what they ought to do or be. Such preaching invariably perverts God's grace into a human achievement, something attained by being nice little boys and girls rather than something that comes as an unmerited gift of God's love. As Keck says, the end result, "tends to be either a distressing trivialization of the Bible into reasonable advice for individuals, or a shrill demanding of absolutes for the church and society."[5]

Moralizing is inimical to the gospel and debilitating to both the pastor's relationship with the people and the goal of Christian preaching. Whether the behavior being urged upon people is the avoidance of the old individualistic smoking-drinking-cursing sins or the new social racism-sexism-nationalism sins makes no difference. It's all the same: the preacher is attempting to scold and berate the congregation by drawing some simple moral inference from the biblical text. But most biblical texts contain moral implications or directives only by secondary inference; their primary purpose is the revelation of God, not the moral direction of humanity. So moral directives are usually only possible through secondary, implied, transferred application of the text. In the Bible, indicative usually precedes imperative; we learn who we are before we learn what we are to do.

Thus Jesus did not preach his Nazareth sermon in Luke 4 to

say, in effect, "All right, gang, let's get out there and liberate the captives and recover sight to the blind"—as worthy as that work might be. Luke recorded it as Jesus' statement of what *he* would do now that the Spirit had anointed *him*. The point of the parable of the prodigal son is not that children ought to obey their parents and not leave home (as I once heard it preached in a sermon), but rather the point is about what God, the parent, is like. Most of these stories and teachings are primarily about God and only secondarily about us.[6] Our human response comes as *response*, as a secondary inference from the primary proclamation.

Once again, this is not to say that the Bible or biblical preaching is without moral or ethical import. It is to say that we must recognize the way in which the Bible itself speaks to ethical concerns and how it is relevant to our ethical questions. A number of years ago, Reinhold Niebuhr spoke of the "fallacy of moralistic preaching." He pointed out that the main problem with such preaching is that people cannot change their behavior simply by being told to change it. This is one of the fundamental insights of all psychology and psychotherapy. In moralistic preaching the preacher is, not a prophet from God, but rather our superego, our Big Daddy (or Big Mamma) telling all us wayward children what we ought to be doing. Gospel becomes law and responsible Christian adults are reduced to dependent children.

The result of such preaching is rarely deeper Christian commitment. On the contrary, it usually fosters either submissive, dependent, childlike ethical weaklings who are dependent on the parent-preacher to tell them what to do (and who then feel guilty and helpless because they cannot do it) or else defensive, hostile, reactionary defenders of their own behavior or ideas who determinedly resist all efforts of the preacher to tell them what to do. Neither response is conducive to courageous Christian engagement with the needs of the world.

People do not change or become involved simply by being told to change or become involved. Nor do they respond to one who speaks to them from the safe and aloof heights of moral superiority. There is a marked difference between the prophet standing under God's Word *with* the people and moralistically delivering God's Word *to* the people.

As John Knox noted some years ago,

> When I was in seminary, we were constantly hearing that the preacher ought to be a prophet. . . . The "prophet" was a preacher whose sermons were almost entirely descriptions and denunciations of social evils—war, inequity in industry, racial discrimination, and the like. These "prophetic" fulminations of the preacher were usually directed, not only at the evils, but also at his congregation—as though these men and women were any more responsible for them than he was! Usually, too he had nothing to propose, whether as a solution of large-scale evils or as a way of life for the individual in the presence of it. And when, for all their patience, the people became tired of coming to church to be fed, and instead of bread receiving stones (even stones thrown at them!) and decided they wanted another preacher, the "prophet" was sure he was a martyr for the truth, a victim of economic and political reaction. Actually, much more often than not, he suffered because he failed to speak as a person to other persons, failed to deal with people where they were . . . , that is, failed to really preach.[7]

We contemporary prophets can guard against moralizing by reminding ourselves of a few important homiletical guides:

1. Stick to the biblical text. The text itself determines the direction and substance of our preaching, not our first notions upon reading the text or any easy moral implications that we draw from the text. The jump from the biblical text to suggestions for contemporary application of it is a long one that should be made with great care.

Here is an experience from my own preaching that shows some of the pitfalls along the road from exegesis to hermeneutics as well as some of the potential prophetic value of disciplining ourselves to take the text to its own terms.

The gospel for the Sunday was Luke 10:1-12, 17-20, Jesus' sending out of the seventy disciples:

> After this the Lord appointed seventy others, and sent them on ahead of him, two by two, into every town and place where he himself was about to come. And he said to them, "The harvest is plentiful, but the laborers are few; pray therefore the Lord of the harvest to send out laborers into this harvest. . . .
>
> The seventy returned with joy, saying, "Lord, even the demons are subject to us in your name!" And he said to them, "I saw Satan fall like lightning from heaven. Behold, I have given you authority to tread upon serpents and scorpions, and over all the power of the enemy; and nothing shall hurt you. Nevertheless do not rejoice in this, that the spirits are subject to you; but rejoice that your names are written in heaven."

Upon my first reading and study of the text, I said to myself, Here is a passage that speaks of the radical quality of discipleship that Jesus demands. It says, "Let the dead bury the dead." It says, Jesus sends out the disciples by telling them that they must risk everything.

Immediately a sermon started coming to mind. Are we really Jesus' disciples today? How willing are we to "let the dead bury the dead"? What would *you* be willing to give up or risk in order to be faithful? How unfaithful our puny discipleship looks when compared to the harsh demands of the gospel! You have heard the sermon before: "Ten Reasons Why You Are Not a Christian."

I was imagining all the prophetic shots I could take during the sermon: "let the dead bury the dead" (versus our conservative, old-fashioned religion); "nowhere to lay your head" (versus our preoccupation with our church buildings); and so on. As I said, you have heard the sermon before.

But I took a closer exegetical look at the text. What is the emotional tone of the text? Joy. What was the overall point of the original setting? Perhaps its point was to encourage a discouraged church. Luke says the Seventy returned with joy (verse 17): "We healed people! It worked! There *is* something to your Lordship after all," they said. And, unlike me, Jesus does not deflate their joy; he confirms it: "Rejoice," he says. "Your names are written in heaven."

My proposed sermon ended with moralizing, guilt building, and defeat. The story itself ends with surprise, joy, and victory. Obviously, my proposed sermon had not been faithful to the text.

So what? What does this message of surprise, joy, and victory—originally spoken to Luke's church—have to do with my church? Why do I want to make Luke's Good News into my church's bad news? I continued to struggle with the question as I went about my pastoral visitation that week. One afternoon I visited a man who had not been in church for a number of years. When he answered the door, I told him that I was his new pastor.

"Did Bentley Hines send you?" he asked after learning who I was. "Bentley has been on my back to get back in church. He has already been here."

Then it hit me. Jesus sent the Seventy "where he himself was about to come." He sent them ahead of him. They were there before he came. They were there as ambassadors who go before the Lord.

Those struggling Christians at Northside Church, for all their faults, were out there ahead of me, maybe even ahead of Christ. They *were* disciples. They *were* healing and conquering. Wonder of wonders, the spirits *are* subject, even to them. At the church clothes closet, at the parties they give at the county prison, as they sit on city council, when they open up their church building to community agencies, when they go out and visit those whom no one else wants to visit—then they are "going where he himself was about to come."

And so my sermon became more congruent with the text. I tasted again some of the surprising joy of the returning Seventy. We do not have to scold, berate, and beg members into ministry. They are already there. (Some do not even know they are there, and so we must tell them.) That ministry must be named and claimed and affirmed as part of the surprising inbreaking of the Kingdom.

And so in my sermon I tried to affirm their ministry:

> Like the Seventy, no one is more surprised than we are when some good comes about through us. Like them, we too come back surprised that someone is healed because of us, some evil is conquered because of us. It never ceases to amaze us that Christ uses even people like us to show his love for the world.

But he does.

> The greatest compliment you could ever receive comes on that day when Christ finally touches someone's life, when the Savior knocks on the door (or kicks it down!), when someone is healed, or forgiven, or given some gift that is only His to give—when that person says to Christ, "Did Bentley Hines send you? Did Bob send you? Or Jane? Or Angie? And Christ will say, "Rejoice," knowing that one of his own has already been where he himself was about to go.

Of course I do not claim that this sermon led people to courageous prophetic action. But I do believe it set the context out of which courageous prophetic action may arise. It did indicate how that action comes about. I also think the sermon rose above the merely moralizing diatribe it threatened to be and became a more faithful witness to the gospel. And faithfulness to the gospel is where truly *Christian* social action arises.

It may also be true, however, that we can preach about nonbiblical ethical issues without giving up the Bible and limiting ourselves to commonly held ethical principles. We Protestants often forget that beyond the text is the gospel tradition, or perhaps more accurately, the gospel and the tradition of the church that inform our decision making in a way that commonly held ethical principles do not.

For instance, I have found it difficult to rely solely on the biblical text for help with thoughts concerning war and the Christian conscience. In preaching about the problem of war, which is a fitting topic for a preacher, I have found it more helpful to appeal to the tradition of the church, or the thought of great Christians from the past and present, or other ecclesial sources in order to put forward a view that, although not exclusively biblical in the narrow sense, at least can claim to be distinctively Christian.

2. As John Knox reminds us, the prophet must remember that all of us, including the prophet, stand under the biblical judgments and demands. "*All* have sinned and fall short of the glory of God (emphasis added)." Prophetic preaching is most believable when the preacher makes clear that he or she is involved in the same ethical dilemmas, the same struggles with the will, the same temptations to moral timidity as other Christians. Such preaching is effective because it is also confessional—and honest.

My first preaching experience was in a family campground ministry one summer while I was in seminary. I preached to vacationers each Sunday while they were away from home. The next summer I happened to run across copies of the sermons I had preached at the campground. I immediately noted that all but a few of them had managed to mention the errors of our involvement in the then-current Vietnam War. No matter what the text or the occasion, somehow I managed to work it around to a fulmination against the war. Why was I so hung upon that one evil? I asked myself. Why would I choose, Sunday after Sunday, to bombard these people, these strangers on vacation, with my criticism of the war? I came to realize that most of those sermons were for *me*, not for them. After all, didn't I take pleasure in bragging to all my friends about how I had been taking a courageous stand against the war? No one could accuse me of cowardice or irrelevance! But whom was I preaching to? Was my goal to speak God's truth or to justify myself?

A little pastoral honesty helps transform trivial moralizing into true prophecy.

3. Related to the example above is the need for pastoral sensitivity in our prophetic preaching; we do not lay aside our pastoral concerns when we assume the prophet's mantle. Such sensitivity is an excellent safeguard against the emotional coercion, moralistic scolding, and simplistic programs offered in much so-called prophetic preaching. Day-to-day, firsthand pastoral involvement with one's people does not so much soften one's prophetic preaching as inform and sharpen it.

In my first parish in rural Georgia I spent much time in sermons berating my people for their racist attitudes. I had been appalled by some of their remarks on black-white relations. Then, after a few months of visiting them in their homes and at their jobs, I realized that my people—uneducated, lower-income, unskilled workers—were the most vulnerable and the most threatened by the influx of black workers into their formerly all-white occupations. It was easy for me to tell them to feel more kindly toward their new black neighbors—I was in a safe, nonthreatened position. So I found that their racism was due more to their fears than to a basic hate for blacks. My discovery did not justify or make right their racism, but it did help me understand their fear better and speak to it more sensitively and relevantly. I then preached less on the need to love and more on how our faith lessens our fears: "perfect love casts out fear."

In other words, I think my prophetic role was sharpened by my pastoral experiences.

CONFRONTATION

In prophetic preaching as in pastoral counseling, one cannot avoid times of confrontation, times when we come face to face with the depth and complexity of our sin and participation in evil both as individuals and as groups. Confrontation is sometimes painful, but it is necessary if we are to encounter the fullness of the gospel. Sometimes the gospel is bad news before it is good news; it hurts before it heals.

As in counseling, confrontation is most effective when it is based upon one's accurate observations of another person's behavior, that is, when it is tied to a discernible reality to which we can point. The role of the prophetic preacher is not so much to pass judgment as to help us see ourselves and our world as it is:

> In the past ten years the population of our town has changed from 30 percent black to 80 percent black. We all know that this is the result, not so much of black people moving in as of white people moving out. Just ten years ago, our own church could count 75 percent of its membership as living within a mile of the church. But now the majority of our members live more than five miles away in the suburbs. We are fleeing, joining the "white flight." What are we running from? What is it we fear? In this sermon I would like to reflect on what I feel are some of your fears and my fears and look honestly at this pressing social problem. . . .

Or,

> The other night in a discussion with our church youth group, I learned something of the scope and depth of the drug problem in our local high school. We haven't done much talking about it. Maybe we don't want to talk about it. I know I don't like to think about it. The thought that our children are exposed daily to such a problem is a thought I wish would simply go away. But we all know it will not go away. Right here in our own town young lives are being

irreparably damaged. Right here in our own schools, young lives are being warped so that they will never live up to their full God-given potential. What can we, as a Christian church, do to respond to this problem?

The prophet refuses to cry "Peace, peace" when there is no peace. The prophet refuses to equate God's ways with our ways. The purpose of our prophetic confrontation in preaching is not to judge or condemn—that business belongs only to God. Our task is to help people see reality as it is. Once they do see it, then change is at last possible. In seeing reality, the choices are laid bare before us. As David Switzer notes, "Confrontation is involved in much of the prophecy of the Old Testament. 'If you do *this*, then *that* will happen.' 'You *say* you worship Yahweh, but you *do* something else.' Or, Nathan to David, 'you agree that this man acted unfairly in the situation described, you have acted precisely the same way.' "[8] Properly understood, confrontation is an expression of love because it seeks to help persons face reality, to enable them to stand before the truth.

When we attempt to protect people from the truth in our preaching, when we attempt to help them weave Pollyanna fantasy worlds, we do them no service. We are helping them be dishonest—not so much out of our pastoral empathy for them as out of our pastoral egotism that leads us to think that we know what is best for them, that they are too fragile to see the truth for themselves, that it is our responsibility to paternalistically shield them from reality. There is not much difference between the egotistical prophet who is always condemning people and telling them what they ought to do, and the egotistical "pastor" who is always soothing people's consciences and telling them that everything is going to be all right and they need not worry.

Consider this example of confrontation that was part of a sermon on Mark 9:33-37, Jesus' words on "whoever receives one such child in my name receives me.":

A nice thought is expressed in this scripture because even if we have a long way to go in our treatment of the poor, the sick, and the oppressed, at least we can take pride that we adults have progressed in our treatment of children. We love children; we receive them.

Well, mostly we receive children.

We read that widespread child abuse exists right here in our own town. "I wish somebody had warned me that children were so selfish and demanding," he said (in the newspaper) as they indicted him for battering in the head of his infant son. Someone should have warned him. Surely Jesus knows that there are limits to how much we are expected to be receptive to children.

"I don't have time to have this baby," she said. "I'm supposed to be in graduate school in the fall." And so she aborted the inconvenience. Should we all be thankful that we now have such freedom of choice? Certainly those words about "receiving children" do not mean we are to receive them even to the point of rearranging our plans and our lives. Working parents, inflation, long weekends, overpopulation, graduate schools, to say nothing of our own adult emotional well-being—all these factors put a strain on our ability to "suffer" the little children.

How many of us are where we are today at the expense of our children? Who made the real sacrifice for us to be here in these homes, in this neighborhood, in this career?

And so yesterday as I struggled with this text, I told my own little one, "Don't bother me now. Can't you see I'm working on a sermon on the necessity of receiving children!"

After all, who do these little ones of ours think we are putting in all those long hours at the job for anyway? Ourselves? When they're older, they'll understand.

A stronger dose of pastoral honesty, in which the pastor asks why he or she is either confronting the people or avoiding confrontation, would be helpful.

But is is not easy. That thing we so easily call truth is as elusive to the pastor as it is to the congregation—perhaps more so. We need discipline and excruciating self-knowledge to preach God's action rather than our program for action. It is easy to confuse our opinions with God's while all the time condemning our people for their opinions.

Above all, integrative prophetic preaching is difficult for pastors simply because they find it difficult to say hard things to those they have learned to love. The young Reinhold Niebuhr discovered this at his first parish in Detroit. After his first few years of trying to combine prophetic preaching and pastoral work, he came to these conclusions about the difficulty of combining the two vocations in one preacher:

> I am not surprised that most prophets are itinerants. Critics of the church think we preachers are afraid to tell the truth because we are economically dependent upon the people of our church. There is something in that, but it does not quite get to the root of the matter. . . . I think the real clue to the tameness of a preacher is the difficulty one finds in telling unpleasant truths to people whom one has learned to love.
>
> To speak the truth in love is a difficult and sometimes an almost impossible, achievement. If you speak the truth unqualifiedly, that is usually because your ire has been aroused or because you have no personal attachment to the object of your strictures. Once personal contact is established you are very prone to temper your wind to the shorn sheep. It is certainly difficult to be human and honest at the same time. I'm not surprised that most budding prophets are tamed in time to become harmless parish priests. [9]

And yet, it is precisely that difficulty—the difficulty of a loving pastor's being forced by the truth to be a courageous prophet—that makes the prophetic preaching of the pastor all the more effective. This is not some "visiting fireman," some outsider who blows through town, blows off steam, and then blows out again. This is their pastor, the one who stands in solidarity with them, the one who knows them and their unique struggles—and they know the pastor and his or her struggles. They cannot so easily dismiss their pastor's prophecy by saying that he or she does not understand the economic, social, or political realities under which they live—because the pastor *knows*. That makes the pastor's prophetic words cut all the more deeply.

Pastoral solidarity with the people may be the most important prophetic necessity—other than the necessity of humble, courageous service to the Word. Niebuhr, after noting the difficulties of combining the pastoral role with the prophetic, says,

> if the Christian adventure is made a *mutual search for truth* in which the preacher is merely a leader among many searchers and is conscious of the same difficulties in his own experience which he notes in others, I do not see why he cannot be a prophet without being forced into itinerancy.[10] (Emphasis added)

VI. THE PREACHER AS LITURGIST

I have seen them there, before the altar of God, hands outstretched, brass plate full of their dollar bills, offering envelopes, and prayer request cards. I have seen them offering up what they had been given, laying it before God and one another. The local auto mechanic passed the plate to the nurse, who passed it to the former school teacher, who passed it to the teen-ager, who gave it to the usher, who, everyday but this one, runs the hardware store downtown. And they sang the doxology and laid it all on the altar.

Praise God from whom all blessings flow!

This offering, this doxology business, is at the heart of liturgy.

I hope by now that we free church Protestants have learned that liturgy is not some high-sounding Latin activity that we leave to others, and that our Roman Catholic brothers and sisters know that it is not some peculiar private possession of those who wear vestments and read prayerbooks.

Liturgy is literally "the work of the people." All Christians do it. At least in the New Testament sense of *leitourgia*, it is all those things Christians do, inside church and outside, for the God they love. Although this work of the people occurs outside the church (in all those acts of loving service Christians do for others because they love God), liturgy occurs most explicitly, most fundamentally, in the service of worship. All our kneeling, praying, singing, shouting, preaching, listening, eating, drinking, washing, and parading about is part of the joyous work we call worship. This final chapter focuses on the integrative function of preaching as an act of worship and the preacher as a leader of worship.[1]

THE SERMON AS AN ACT OF WORSHIP

As the people offer up their money, prayers, bread and wine, hopes and fears, doubts and praise, they ask the priest or pastor to offer a sermon. The sermon is the preacher's service. It is service that is sometimes a gift: the gift of healing, sustaining, guiding, encouraging the people. It is also service that is sometimes a burden: the burden of witnessing to the truth, speaking like a prophet, saying the things that are not pleasant to hear.

But whether it is experienced on any given Sunday as a burden or as a blessing, the sermon is always an act of worship. As John Knox says,

> Unless we conceive of preaching as being itself an act of worship, we miss what is most essential in it and what distinguishes it most radically from other kinds of teaching, religious or secular. The real truth of the matter is not that preaching merely happens usually to be set in a context of worship or that it is most effective when it has that kind of setting. Rather, it cannot be really preaching except in that context. If the context of worship is not there already, the true sermon creates it. Either preaching contributes to, provides a medium of worship, or it is not preaching at all.[2]

Knox sees the liturgical character of a sermon most clearly in the preparation of the sermon. A sermon should be prepared, he says, as an act of worship, the offering of the preacher, a prayer.

> The sermon is an offering to God—or rather it is the preacher offering himself to God—and the preparation is a disciplined act of devotion. To preach is really to pray with others, to lead others in prayer; to prepare to preach is, certainly under one important aspect, to pray for others and for oneself for the sake of others. [3]

Understanding the sermon as an act of worship has far-reaching consequences related to the nature of worship. Christian worship has its primary focus in the praise and adoration of God; all other activity is secondary to our response to a loving Creator. Worship has no more worthy purpose than the proclamation, praise, and adoration of God. Whenever worship is used for some other purpose—worthy though it may be—it is being used and thereby abused. The focus of worship is *God*, not us. Whenever we use worship to educate, titillate, soothe, anger, instruct, judge, or do other things to people, the primary focus of worship has shifted from God to us.

This is not to say that worship has no human consequences. While we are praising God, we often find that something happens to us. Sometimes, we are educated, titillated, soothed, angered, instructed, or judged. But all these come as a result of focusing our affections upon God, as a by-product of worship. The main thing that happens to us in worship and the primary reason we keep doing it is that we are brought close to God.

Some of us who orchestrate and concoct services of worship that are designed on the basis of how effectively they move the congregation from point A to point B need to ask ourselves, Who is worship for anyway? Whenever we are the center of our worship, the final test for its faithfulness, or the goal toward which all its activity moves, we are doing something other than worshiping God.

What does this mean for preaching? I find it helpful to think of sermons, in their various forms, as various acts of worship.

Some sermons are doxologies—because there is truth that is preached best by being sung. Some sermons are prayers—because the preacher is speaking as much of *our* needs as of your needs. Some are like the Eucharist—because the preacher is but one hungry person telling other hungry persons where to find bread. Some are pure credo—bold affirmation of the truth we hold and the truth that holds us. All sermons are oblation: offering what we have before God who takes it, blesses it, and gives it to feed the hungry multitudes.

Thinking of the sermon as an act of worship has some immediate practical consequences. For one thing, it reminds us that a sermon is as much something that we do as something we say. Contemporary worship renewal has noted that worship is more a series of actions than a set of words. In the centuries after the Reformation, many churches fell into worship patterns that were mostly words: the pastor's duty was mostly to speak and the congregation's duty was mostly to listen. Prayerbooks, printed bulletins, and hymnals—all inventions of the Gutenberg printing revolution—reinforced the notion that words were more important in worship than deeds.

Now we are learning again to trust the power of the symbolic, the efficacy of the visual. We are learning again the joy of focusing our attention upon the ordinary stuff of everyday life and seeing God revealed in it—in the bread and wine, the water, a handshake, a kiss, an embrace. Many of us worship leaders, therefore, are having to correct old habits. Presiding in the liturgy requires sensitivity to body language—what we say by how we do things.

Like every other aspect of liturgical leadership, preaching is a visual as well as an auditory experience. Our sermons must be prepared not only by paying attention to what we say but also by paying attention to how we say it. A mirror and tape recorder can be as helpful here as a lectionary and commentary. Honest observers who carefully watch how we do things in our preaching and then tell us what they see can also be helpful. We do little good if we speak of grace and then appear to be ungracious in the way we invite persons to the Communion table, or hand them bread, or greet them at the end of the worship.

For some time now we have criticized the old oratorical, rhetorical style of preaching of the past. Bombastic oratory is probably inappropriate for most Christian communication. One has to admit, however, that many preachers of a bygone era were sensitive to the visual aspects of public speaking in a way that we are not.

Read Spurgeon's *Lectures to My Students* and note the detailed instructions he gives for body gestures. A minister who drools into the microphone, hides behind the pulpit, mumbles and slurs words, or slouches at the altar cheapens the message. We do not put our hands in our pockets when we say something important. We do not shout and flail our arms in the air when we offer consolation. As one person said of her pastor, "He has no sense of occasion. His sermons are all warm fireside chats at which he smiles and talks softly—regardless of the text, the season, or the occasion. This is as inappropriate as if he screamed at us in every sermon." Our gestures, movement, posture, and facial expression should be appropriate. Actions do speak louder than words.

Using intentional, firm, confident gestures helps make the congregation comfortable because then persons know someone is in charge who feels good about leading them, and attractive, neat, and colorful vestments help set the tone for the assembly.

But a pastor's eyes are the principal means of communicating with and leading the congregation. When the choir sings, therefore, the leader's eyes should be on them. When a lay reader is reading the scripture, the pastor's eyes should be on that person. When the pastor gives bread to a person in the

Eucharist, he or she should establish eye contact and hold it while placing the bread in the communicant's hand. During periods of silence—all too infrequent in most of our services—the minister can help the congregation focus inwardly by focusing his or her eyes, settling into a comfortable but not slouching posture, and using the silence for real reflection.

All these gestures help proclaim the gospel as vividly and pointedly as any words we may speak. The sermon is an *act* of worship.

We can also avoid a host of homiletical sins by preparing the sermons as if we were preparing a liturgical activity. Some time ago one of my evangelical friends said, "All preaching must lead to response." But if all preaching is designed to elicit some kind of concrete response, then it cannot always be biblical preaching (unless we define *response* so broadly that the word loses its meaning). Numerous portions of Scripture do not call a response—except a loud amen. For example, what kind of response does this passage evoke: "O the depth of the riches and wisdom and knowledge of God! How unsearchable are his judgments and how inscrutable his ways! (Romans 11:33).

Much biblical truth is meant simply to be affirmed as true, to be adored rather than acted upon. Much of it is truth about who God is rather than what we are to do. It is truth that, as in any act of worship, is to be sung, shouted, adored, or quietly reflected upon. When preaching on this kind of truth, the preacher simply proclaims reality: the way things are, what God has done and is doing.

Certainly such truth has ethical implications. A song, a poem, an hour of quiet meditation, a vision of reality—even the impact of a pastor's personality—may lead to changed lives, courageous action, or heroic commitment. But such response comes as *response* to the truth, to our vision of the way things are in this world now that God has gotten into the act.

One of the most difficult things in worship is for the leader to lead without getting in the way, so to speak. In our protest against some of the inhuman, robotlike liturgical leadership of the past, some of us overreact. We turn worship into a folksy, preacher-directed hour in which the congregation is treated to the innermost thoughts and aspirations of the pastor, or to jokes, or to warm moments, or to prophetic ravings—depending on the pastor's personality and theological inclinations. Sometimes people complain that they cannot see God for looking at the pastor!

Ours is a difficult task: to convey sensitivity, warmth, and care in our liturgical leadership and still provide a setting whereby worshipers are enabled to see through us to God. Only a thin line separates the facilitating of congregational worship from becoming the center of worship. Sometimes we do not know when we do overstep that line; then an honest friend can help us evaluate our public worship-leadership style.

I like to use the analogy of a chairperson at a meeting. The best chairpersons move us along to our common goal without obstructing our movement by taking over the meeting. Their main function is to call the group's attention to what needs to be done, help the group listen to itself, then move the meeting to its conclusion. They trust the group and its resources.

When our sermons center on "The Life and Struggles of Pastor X," we are in danger of turning the sermons into performances rather than oblations. The history of worship warns us against the human tendency to make worship into a drama for the faithful: the faith is always to be lived, not merely watched. When we see the sermon as a tool to get people to do this or that—no matter how beneficial to them or the church—proclamation has degenerated into manipulation and the worship of God into a technique for motivating people. Then the sermon attends, not to the mystery of God, but to the self-evident, the trite, the didactic. It lapses into humanistic platitudes and simplistic solutions for the human plight, and boredom is the inevitable result.

Trusting the Word and trusting persons to hear and respond to the Word in their own way are part of a basic respect for persons and for the Word of God that enables worship to take place.

Like any good liturgy, thoughtful sermons are an invitation to risk meeting and being met by God—no matter what the consequences. We cannot force that meeting in liturgy or in preaching. We cannot determine in advance what the consequences of such a meeting will be. We can only call persons to the meeting, help focus their attention, set the context in which the meeting may happen, and give participants space to follow the Spirit. This is the goal in planning preaching or worship.

WORSHIP AS THE SETTING FOR THE SERMON

We have said that the sermon is an act of worship and the gospel is proclaimed in both word and deed. At one time we Protestants saw the sermon as *the* act of worship; all else in the service was a preliminary to the preaching. But now new patterns of worship within most mainline Protestant denominations as well as renewed understandings of the purpose of Sunday morning have brought things into better balance. Word *and* the Sacrament are the two historic foci for Sunday worship.[4]

I think of the relationship between the sermon and the Lord's Supper this way: The Eucharist is primarily an eschatological, ecstatic experience. It provides a time apart. The meal is a foretaste of the banquet in the Kingdom. In this time of eating and drinking with Christ, our eyes are opened and we see the hungry multitudes coming and being filled, we see sinners at the gospel feast, we welcome these strangers as our brothers and sisters. The presence of the risen Christ is made real, and we glimpse the promised "new heaven and new earth" (Rev. 21:1*a*)

All this can and often does happen when we celebrate the Lord's Supper. It is therefore a joyous, healing, resurrection occasion. But in the midst of this joy and thanksgiving for God's victory in Christ, the sermon says, "Yes—but not yet."

The sermon is therefore a contemporaneous reminder that we still live between the times, stretched between the now of life in this world and the not-yet of God's complete redemption of the world. The decisive victory has been won, but many battles remain to be fought. The sermon often speaks of those battles. It points to the reality of a creation that still groans in travail as it awaits redemption. It speaks of the Monday-morning blues, of cornflakes at breakfast, of the cancer that will not heal, of the marriage that will not last, and of the oppression that goes on and on. The sermon is bitingly, pointedly, specifically contemporary in the midst of our Eucharistic remembrance and foretaste. It reminds us that we are brothers and sisters in Christ—but not yet. We are redeemed—but not yet. God rules over all—but not yet. The hungry are being filled with good things—but not yet.

Without a good, cold dose of the preached Word, therefore, the Eucharist can become a detached fantasy trip that is more an attempt at magic than a Christian sacrament. Paul had to tell the Corinthians (1 Cor. 11-12) that their lack of love had made their Eucharist a mockery. Paul's homiletical realism is a much-needed corrective for any church that prematurely announces the advent of the Kingdom at its table.

On the other hand, sermons without the Eucharist threaten to overwhelm the congregation by listing human failures without celebrating God's victory. Without this sacrament the sermon tends always to say, "No, no, not yet." The word is spoken but not enacted. The vision is sketched, sometimes in vivid words, but never embodied in bread and wine. The presence of the risen Christ is pointed to but never touched.

Prophetic or judgmental sermons leave the congregation to wallow in the mire of all the things it is not, rather than moving on to celebrate who, by God's grace, it is. And affirming and encouraging sermons frustrate the congregation because it is never able to act upon what it feels: an invitation to the feast is given but the feast is left uneaten.

Protestant worship renewal will have succeeded only when persons leave church on Sunday morning and say to their pastor, "That was such a wonderful sermon. It's a shame we have to go home now and eat alone when we could have eaten together at the Lord's Table." These people know, in their heart of hearts, that being Christian is more than hearing a good sermon, singing a good hymn, and then going home to eat a good dinner. How those of us who are heirs of the evangelical tradition could forget that the sermon is an invitation to the gospel feast is one of the most distressing mysteries of church history.

Yet with my free-church heritage, I can still affirm that the sermon is at the center of Sunday morning worship, for it can be at the center without being the climax. The reading and preaching of God's Word can be the central point toward which the first acts of worship move and from which later acts flow.

This centrality is mainly a structural matter. When planning our pattern of worship, we need to ask, What do we need to do to gather to hear God's Word? Worship-planners are taking seriously the need for a time of gathering in the service. Informal and formal greetings, welcome of visitors, announcements, rehearsal of new music—all are appropriate activities during the gathering. From the gathering, all hymns, prayers, and responses before the scripture reading and the sermon should be seen as *preparation* for hearing. Such gathering and preparation assume that we need to prepare our congregation's own individual hearts and minds for the word. None of us knows how many sermons fall on deaf ears for lack of adequate congregational participation.

Likewise, all acts that follow the reading and preaching can be seen as fitting responses to the word. For many of us this means planning more acts of worship to come after the sermon. A creed, the offering, prayers of thanksgiving and intercession, baptism, and the Lord's Supper are best seen as response to the word.[5] As we noted earlier, most of our services lack sufficient opportunity for a variety of congregational response. The word seems to fall on deaf ears. We preach the word—but then we do nothing. Rising to our feet after the sermon with a hearty "This we believe . . . ," coming forward for baptism or for the Lord's Supper, and praying for the needs of the world are most effective as postsermon responses. In this way our liturgy becomes a symbol for the way we experience the Christian life inside and outside the church: hearing the word, being touched by the truth, then responding to that revelation in word and deed. When this happens, liturgy is life, the word becomes flesh in our lives, and the integration that is at the heart of faith itself occurs.

In the moments before the sermon you wait silently as the last notes of the organ sound and you look out upon the flock that now waits upon the word. You see Martha Jones, who stopped you on your way out of the study to tell you she doesn't like the way you spoke to her daughter last week during the church picnic. What her daughter does with her time is her daughter's business—not yours or anybody else's—she says. Then, scarcely ten steps down the hall, Jack Gibbes said something to you about a disturbing aspect of his yearly physical and asked you to pray for him. You caught a glimpse of two teen-agers sneaking out to the parking lot to skip your sermon. You overheard a couple in the narthex talking about no one's speaking to them when they visited last

Sunday. And all this is with you now, in spite of your efforts to lay it aside so you can preach. But you cannot lay it aside, and so you gather it up in your arms and hold it close to you.

The text for today . . . You gave it your best effort, consulted the commentary—but got little help there. Perhaps you are planning to say too much. Perhaps you have twisted the meaning of the text to what you want it to say to these sinners. Or perhaps you are saying too little, shielding people from the harsh truth of the text.

You are not sure. But it's too late for that now. For as the last notes of music die away and people settle back in their seats, you walk to the pulpit. You open the Bible and begin to read, wondering through the words that flow from the text what will happen to your words. What good will this do? What harm will it do? Whose life will it affect? What demons will be set in motion once the word is turned loose in their hearts? What will happen to you—or in you?

It is too late for that now. All that is left is for you to speak. And for the hundredth time, in spite of all the questions that have no answers, in spite of all the misgivings, the doubts, the lack of answers, you do speak. For the hundredth Sunday you take all those feelings, doubts, questions, all the confusion, the unknowing, and the faith—you lay them all upon the altar, before God and everyone else. You know this is not the best sermon that could be preached, but it is the only one you have today. You know you cannot say all that could be said, but it is all that will be said here today. You know you are not the best of preachers, but you are the best your congregation has now.

So you speak. You never cease to be amazed that you have the courage to speak. You wonder how you have the nerve to do it. But your flock have offered themselves—given God what they have—so now you give what you have. You take it all and lay it upon the altar as your gift, your offering, your oblation. You set it there before them while you sing both a Kyrie—"Lord, have mercy. . . .

Christ, have mercy . . ."—and a doxology. And you speak. You dare to speak. You dare to lay your offering before them. And because you do, the word is let loose, the Spirit starts to rove among them, the bread is broken and passed around, and, for better or worse, the gospel feast begins again. For the millionth time in our story, God's people hear the word, and they are fed.

NOTES

CHAPTER I

1) Harry Emerson Fosdick, *The Living of These Days* (New York:Harper & Brothers, 1956), p. 94.

2) Karl Barth, *The Preaching of the Gospel*, trans. B.E. Hooke (Philadelphia: Westminster Press, 1963), p. 53.

3) Ronald E. Sleeth, *Proclaiming the Word* (Nashville: Abingdon Press, 1964), p. 98.

4) Fred B. Craddock, *As One Without Authority* (Nashville: Abingdon, 1979), pp. 82-83.

5) Barth, *Preaching*, p. 53.

6) In my book (with Robert Wilson) *Preaching and Worship in the Small Church* (Nashville: Abingdon, 1980), I more fully develop my personal prejudice that large, multithousand-member congregations are an inadequate setting for Christian preaching and worship.

7) James Cleland, *The True and Lively Word* (New York: Charles Scribner's Sons, 1954), pp. 73-74.

8) Søren Kierkegaard, *Point of View for My Work as an Author*, trans. Walter Lowrie (New York: Harper and Row, 1962), p. 27.

9) Leander Keck, *The Bible in the Pulpit* (Nashville, Abingdon, 1978), p. 15.

10) Ronald Sleeth, "The Crisis in Preaching," *Perkins Journal*, XXX, No. 4 (Summer 1977), p. 11.

11) Frederick Buechner, *Telling the Truth* (New York: Harper & Row, 1977), pp. 22-23.

CHAPTER II

1) These four pastoral activities are the four historic functions of pastoral care as delineated in Charles R. Jaeckle and William A. Clebsch's *Pastoral Care in Historical Perspective*, (Englewood Cliffs, N.J.: Prentice-Hall, 1964), pp. 34-66.

2) See my *Worship As Pastoral Care* (Nashville: Abingdon, 1979), Chaps. I and II; also my book (with John H. Westerhoff, III) *Liturgy and Learning Through the Life Cycle* (New York: Seabury Press, 1980).

3) Don S. Browning, *The Moral Context of Pastoral Care* (Philadelphia: Westminster Press, 1976).

4) David K. Switzer, *Pastor, Preacher, Person* (Nashville: Abingdon, 1979), p. 52.

5) Arthur L. Teikmanis, *Preaching and Pastoral Care* (Englewood Cliffs, N.J.: Prentice-Hall, 1964), p. 19.

6) Quoted in "Preaching in Pastoral Perspective," in Edmund A. Steimle, *et al.*, *Preaching the Story* (Philadelphia: Fortress Press, 1980), p. 109.

7) Søren Kierkegaard, *Concluding Scientific Postscript* (Princeton, N.J.: Princeton University Press, pp. 415-16.

8) See, for instance, Paul W. Pruyser, *The Minister as Diagnostician* (Philadelphia: Westminster Press, 1976); Browning, *The Moral Context of Pastoral Care*; and my own *Worship as Pastoral Care*.

CHAPTER III

1) Seward Hiltner, *Ferment in the Ministry* (Nashville: Abingdon Press, 1969), p. 58.

2) James D. Glasse, *Profession: Minister* (Nashville: Abingdon Press, 1968).

3) Urban T. Holmes, *The Future Shape of Ministry* (New York: The Seabury Press, 1971), pp. 27, 31.

4) Switzer, *Pastor, Preacher, Person*, p. 19.

5) Willimon, *Worship as Pastoral Care*, pp. 198-99.

6) *Ibid.*, pp. 202-3.

7) *Ibid.*, pp. 203-4.

8) I have described these factors in more detail in my section (chapter 4) of Robert L. Wilson's *Shaping the Congregation* (Nashville: Abingdon, 1980).

9) Switzer, *Pastor, Preacher, Person*, p. 20.

10) Glenn E. Whitlock, *Preventive Psychology and the Church* (Philadelphia: Westminster Press, 1973), p. 18.

11) Switzer, *Pastor, Preacher, Person*, p. 20.

12) Barth, *Preaching of the Gospel*, p. 31.

13) P.T. Forsyth quoted in *Preaching in the Witnessing Community*, ed. Herman G. Stuempfle, Jr. (Philadelphia: Fortress Press, 1973), p. viii.

14) Richard John Neuhaus, *Freedom for Ministry* (New York: Harper & Row, 1979), p. 143.

CHAPTER IV

1) Dean M. Kelley, *Why Conservative Churches Are Growing* (New York: Harper & Row, 1972).

2) C. H. Dodd, *The Apostolic Preaching and Its Development* (New York: Harper & Row, 1936).

3) Definition adapted from Gwen K. Neville and John H. Westerhoff, *Learning through Liturgy* (New York: Seabury Press, 1978), p. 93. For an exploration of the many ways people learn while they worship, see Westerhoff and Willimon, *Liturgy and Learning.*

4) Colin Morris, *The Word and the Words* (Nashville: Abingdon Press, 1975), pp. 29-30.

5) Gerhard Ebeling, *Theology and Proclamation*, trans. John Riches (Philadelphia: Fortress Press, 1966), p. 20.

6) Washington Gladden, *The Christian Pastor* (1898), Charles F. Kemp, *Pastoral Preaching* (St. Louis, Missouri: Bethany Press, 1963), p. 239.

CHAPTER V

1) See Catherine Gunsalus González and Justo Luis González, *Liberation Preaching: The Pulpit and the Oppressed* (Nashville: Abingdon, 1980).

2) Jürgen Moltmann, "Christian Theology Today," *New World Outlook*, No. 62 (1972), pp. 483-90.

3) William H. Willimon with Robert Wilson, *Preaching and Worship in the Small Church* (Nashville: Abingdon, 1980), pp. 104-5.

4) Leander E. Keck, *The Bible in the Pulpit* (Nashville: Abingdon, 1978), p. 102.

5) *Ibid.*, p. 105.

6) Elsewhere I have called this the "theocentric" approach to biblical interpretation in preaching. I develop these thoughts in more detail in my *The Sustaining Presence: New Testament Worship* (Valley Forge, Pennsylvania: Judson Press, 1981), chapter 6.

7) John Knox, *The Integrity of Preaching* (Nashville: Abingdon Press, 1957), p. 72.

8) David Switzer, *Pastor, Preacher, Person*, p. 91.

9) Reinhold Niebuhr, *Leaves from the Notebook of a Tamed Cynic* (New York: Meridian Books, 1957), pp. 74-75.

10) *Ibid.*, p. 75.

CHAPTER VI

1) For a full treatment of preaching as liturgical activity see William Skudlarek's *The Word in Worship: Preaching in a Liturgical Context* (Nashville: Abingdon, 1981).

2) John Knox, *The Integrity of Preaching*, p. 76.

3) *Ibid.*

4) See *Word and Table* (Nashville: Abingdon 1976).

5) For this reason, when a number of ministers are present at the Eucharistic celebration, the person who preaches should also be the one who presides at the table and prays the Eucharistic prayer.

SUGGESTIONS FOR FURTHER READING

Jabusch, Willard F. *The Person in the Pulpit: Preaching as Caring.* Nashville: Abingdon, 1980.

Keck, Leander E. *The Bible in the Pulpit.* Nashville: Abingdon, 1978.

Kemp, Charles F., ed. *Pastoral Preaching.* St. Louis, Missouri: Bethany Press, 1963.

Kemp, Charles F., ed. *The Preaching Pastor.* St. Louis, Missouri: Bethany Press, 1966.

Killinger, John. *The Centrality of Preaching.* Waco, Texas: Word Books, 1969.

Skudlarek, William, OSB. *The Word in Worship: The Liturgical Context of Preaching.* Nashville: Abingdon, 1980.

Switzer, David. *Pastor, Preacher, Person.* Nashville: Abingdon, 1979.

Teikmanis, Arthur L. *Preaching and Pastoral Care.* Philadelphia: Fortress Press, 1964.

Willimon, William H. *Worship as Pastoral Care.* Nashville: Abingdon, 179.

————— and Wilson, Robert L. *Preaching and Worship in the Small Church.* Nashville: Abingdon, 1980.

INDEX OF SUBJECTS AND AUTHORS

INDEX OF SCRIPTURE REFERENCES